DARE TO BE A CEO

TURNING SETBACKS INTO A LIFE OF SUCCESS

JOEY D. RENDON

ISBN

Hardcase 979-8-89777-350-3
Paperback 979-8-89724-977-0

Dedication

To my beloved late grandparents, **Maximo Sr. and Cristita Domingo**, whose legacy of love and wisdom continues to guide me.

To my cherished late parents, **Nita and Nelson Rendon**, whose sacrifices and unwavering support shaped the person I am today.

To my dear siblings, in-laws, nieces, and nephews—**Novelyn, Niel, May, Dave, Nelson Jr., Dan Rodney, and Jenilyn**—your love and encouragement have been my foundation.

To my beloved wife, **Thirdly**, my partner in life and love, whose presence makes every challenge worth facing and every victory more meaningful.

To my **Discipleship Family—Team Tubay, Team Alfaro, Team Ormeo, Team Castillo, Team Tamayo**, and the entire **Christ Commission Fellowship** community—who walk alongside me and my wife in faith, purpose, and unwavering devotion.

To my best friend, **Divash, and his family**, for their steadfast friendship and unwavering belief in me throughout my journey.

To all my **fervent prayer partners**, especially my **beloved spiritual mum, Dr. Minnie Hill**, and my **brother in faith, Prakash Thing, his wife Merry, and their children**—your prayers, wisdom, and love have been a source of strength and grace in my life.

Above all, all glory and honor belong to **Jesus Christ alone,** who is my greatest source of **strength and wisdom.** It is through Him that I find the courage to persevere, the wisdom to navigate challenges, and the faith to keep pressing forward.

This book is a tribute to all of you—my guiding lights, my strength, and my inspiration.

Contents

Prologue: The Moment That Changed Everything

"Success is not final, failure is not fatal: it is the courage to continue that counts." – Winston Churchill

A Reflection on Resilience

This quote is a powerful reminder that both success and failure are temporary. Neither defines us—what truly matters is how we respond to each moment of triumph or defeat. Life's most defining moments are not the ones where we win but the ones where we refuse to let failure break us.

There are moments that force us to make a choice—moments where we stand at a crossroads between giving up and fighting back. These moments shape our future, revealing who we truly are and what we are capable of becoming.

For me, that moment came when I found myself at rock bottom.

Losing Everything

I had always believed in hard work, seizing opportunities, and building a future that would provide not only for me but also for those who believed in me. I thought I was on the right path.

Then, everything collapsed.

The gold scheme in Qatar, in which I had invested with full confidence, turned out to be a disaster. I had poured my time, resources, and trust into something that crumbled before my eyes, shattering my sense of security, reputation, and confidence.

I wasn't just facing financial ruin—I was mentally and emotionally drained.

People I trusted disappeared. Promises faded into silence. My name, once associated with opportunity, was now a warning. I had to face the painful reality that I had not only lost money but also trust—both in others and in myself.

The weight of failure was suffocating.

I had 2 choices:

✓Accept defeat and let failure define me.
✓ Rise up, rebuild, and prove that setbacks are just setups for a greater comeback.

I chose the Later.

The Turning Point

That moment forced me to look deep within myself. It redefined my mindset, forcing me to question everything I thought I knew about success. I realized something crucial:

Success is not about never failing. It is about rising each time you fall.

Failure is not a full stop—it is a comma, a pause, a redirection toward something greater.

I refused to let that moment define the rest of my life. Instead, I used it as a lesson, a foundation for something stronger, something unbreakable.

Everything I've built since then—the businesses, the networks, the leadership roles—has been rooted in that defining moment. It was the moment I made a decision:

I would take full ownership of my life.
I would stop waiting for things to change.
I would start acting like the CEO of my own destiny.

Why This Book Exists

This book is for those who have faced setbacks.

For those who have felt lost, stuck, or unsure of what's next.

For those who have dared to dream but need a blueprint to turn those dreams into reality.

I know what it's like to feel as if life has knocked you down one too many times. To feel like you've given everything you had, only to watch it slip away. I know the pain of failure, the shame of disappointment, and the fear of starting over.

But I also know this:

You are stronger than you think.
You are capable of more than you realize.
You have the power to rise, to rewrite your story, and to turn your struggles into stepping stones for success.
Your past does not define you—your choices do.
Your failures are not meant to break you but to build you.

Becoming the CEO of Your Own Life

People often associate the term "CEO" with running a company. But being a CEO is not just about business—it is a mindset.

Being the CEO of your life means:

Taking full responsibility for your future.
Refusing to let external circumstances control your destiny.
Learning from failures instead of being paralyzed by them.
Creating opportunities instead of waiting for them.

The truth is, no one is coming to save you. No one is going to build your dreams for you. No one can take control of your future—except you. It's time to stop waiting for the perfect moment. The perfect moment is now. It's time to stop hoping for things to change. *You* are the change you've been waiting for. It's time to stop fearing failure. Every setback is a setup for something greater.

Your Transformation Begins NOW

The most powerful decision you will ever make is to take full ownership of your life.

Not tomorrow. Not next week. But today.

This book is not just about success. It is about resilience, reinvention, and the courage to rise after every fall.

Let this book serve as your guide—a roadmap to rebuilding, redefining, and reclaiming your power.

You are not here by accident.
You were meant for more.
Your journey to transformation begins now.
Are you ready?
Let's go.

Introduction: The Life You Create

"The only way to do great work is to love what you do." – Steve Jobs

Reflection: Passion fuels perseverance. If you love what you do, even the hardest days feel purposeful. When we align our work with our passions, it transforms from a job into a fulfilling mission.

Life is not easy. I learned this at a young age. I grew up knowing what struggle felt like—understanding that nothing would ever be handed to me. But along the way, I also learned something even more powerful: **You don't have to accept life as it is—you can create the life you desire.**

Looking back, my journey has been shaped by 2 things: **the people who believed in me and the choices I made to keep moving forward.**

I could have stayed in my small village, surrounded by people who thought life was just about surviving. But I wanted more. **I refused to let my circumstances define my future.** I looked beyond my surroundings, learned from those ahead of me, and made bold moves—even when I was afraid.

One of the biggest lessons I've learned is this:

You must choose your environment wisely.
You must surround yourself with people who challenge and inspire you.

If the people around you are not contributing to your growth, you must have the courage to step away.

This book is not just about my story—it's about the lessons, failures, turning points, and mindset shifts that helped me break free from limitations. I want to take you on this journey so you can see that no matter where you come from or **what obstacles you face, you have the power to create a different life.**

As you read this book, I encourage you to ask yourself:

Am I truly creating the life I desire?
Am I surrounding myself with people who push me toward growth?
Am I willing to make bold decisions to change my future?

Because **success is not about luck.**
It's about choice.

It's time to **Dare to be a CEO—**of **your own life.**

Chapter 1

The Seed of a Dream

"Dreams don't work unless you do." – John C. Maxwell

Reflection: Having big dreams is important, but action and persistence are what turn dreams into reality. Fear of failure should never hold us back from taking that first step.

"No dream is too big when you have the courage to ask."

Let me tell you a little about my family. We were a humble household of 8 siblings, and I was the fourth among them. Our home was a 30-minute walk from school, and though we lived with very little, we grew up happy, surrounded by the love of our grandparents and parents.

My mother and I were partners—not just in life but in survival. We planted vegetables and sold them, a skill I learned from her. She was the hardest-working woman I have ever known. If I could give her an award, she would have been named **"The Best Mother Ever."** She washed clothes, ironed them, and even worked for our school principal and teachers to make ends meet.

During recognition days and graduations, she would borrow clothes from kind neighbors so that we could look presentable—buying new ones was never an option. I still remember my school bag; it wasn't a real bag at all, just a simple fishnet. Our lunch was wrapped in banana leaves—a reminder of how resourceful we had to be.

Mealtime was sacred in our home. We didn't have much, so we had to stretch what we had. My mother would grate cassava, remove its juice, and dry it before placing it on top of the rice. The young ones were given rice, while the older siblings ate mostly cassava. Many times, my mother didn't eat at all. Instead, she sipped **"rice coffee"**—burned rice boiled in water until it turned black, a substitute for the real thing.

Looking back, those days make me miss her even more—the simple life, eating side by side, sleeping close together. It was a tough life, but it was ours.

The Day That Changed Everything

I was **9 years old** when I first learned that survival wasn't just about strength; it was about finding the right people to believe in you.

One morning, as the scent of dew filled the air, I walked barefoot along the dirt road, my heart pounding with both fear and hope. That day, I wasn't just going to school. I was about to ask for something that could change my life.

We had no money to pay for my education, and I knew my time in school was running out. But I wasn't ready to give up. With trembling hands, I knocked on the doors of 2 women who held the power to decide my future—**my principal, Ms Reyes, and my teacher, Ms Zulueta.**

"Ma'am, can I work for you in exchange for my school fees?" My voice was small, but my determination was loud.

For a moment, there was silence. My mother stood beside me, her eyes filled with quiet resignation. We had no other options. But then, something incredible happened—**Ms Reyes smiled, and Ms Zulueta nodded.**

And just like that, I was given a chance.

The Work That Taught Me Everything

From that day on, my mornings started long before the school bell rang. I fed pigs, chickens, goats, and buffaloes. I swept floors, cooked food, and did every chore I could. It was exhausting, but I didn't mind.

Because I wasn't just working—I was earning something far greater than money.

I was getting an education.

It was then that I learned my first **lesson about leadership:**

Opportunities are given to those who dare to ask, but they are sustained by those who work for them.

Reflections from Ms. Reyes and Ms. Zulueta

"Even as a child, Joey had something special—a determination that set him apart. We knew he was different, and we knew he would go far."

That first chance led to many others. Little did I know that this was just the beginning of a journey where people would continue stepping in, guiding me, lifting me, and believing in me.

Key Lessons from Chapter 1

1. **Courage Opens Doors** – Asking for opportunities, even in fear, can change your life.
2. **Hard Work Sustains Success** – Opportunities are given to those who dare to ask but are kept by those who work for them.
3. **The Right People Can Shape Your Future** – Finding the right mentors and supporters can make all the difference.

Chapter 2

Breaking Free – Choosing a Different Life

"Do not go where the path may lead, go instead where there is no path and leave a trail." – Ralph Waldo Emerson

A Reflection on Breaking Free

Choosing a different path requires stepping out of your comfort zone. It means embracing uncertainty, taking risks, and creating opportunities where none seem to exist. Many people stay where they are, not because they lack potential but because they fear the unknown. The greatest lesson I've learned is that growth does not happen where it is comfortable—it happens when you decide to **move**, even when the destination is unclear.

The First Step Toward Change

"You are not stuck. You are just surrounded by the wrong mindset."

At 12 years old, I moved out of my childhood home. Not because I wanted to but because I had to.

I loved my family, but I knew that if I stayed, my opportunities would be limited. My education depended on this difficult decision. I had already learned that life wasn't going to be easy, but this was the moment I realized something deeper:

If I wanted to build a better future, I couldn't stay in the same place, surrounded by the same limitations.

This was a lesson I would carry with me for the rest of my life.

New Home, New Lesson

When I started living with **Manang Juvy and Manong Berting Sayco**, my life was once again shaped by service.

I cooked, cleaned, and tutored their children.
I helped with household chores in exchange for a roof over my head.
I enrolled at **Lopez Jaena National High School** with hope in my heart.

At first, I thought this was just another chapter of hardship. But I soon realized it was more than that—it was an opportunity to grow, to observe, to learn.

Living in different households exposed me to new ways of thinking, new family structures, and new perspectives on life. It was during this time that I learned another important lesson:

If you want a different life, you must expose yourself to different environments.

I wasn't just learning from books; I was learning from the way people lived.

Some families were generous.
Some were strict.
Some were inspiring.
Some were trapped in the same struggles as my own.

I paid attention. I took mental notes. And I started to understand something powerful:

I didn't want to just survive. I wanted to create a life that would allow me to thrive.

Finding Purpose in Service

When my time with the Sayco family ended, I moved into a new household—this time with **Pastor Artemio Magallanes and his wife, Helen.**

Here, my responsibilities went beyond just housework:

I took care of their children.
I cleaned their home.
I washed clothes and cooked meals.

But what impacted me the most was my involvement in the **church**.

I wasn't just working for my survival anymore—I was **serving**. I was contributing to something greater than myself. It was in the church that I found strength through **faith**. My struggles started to feel like more than just challenges; they felt like a **calling**. It was then that I first felt the **desire to help others grow**. Watching our pastor guide his congregation made me see that leadership wasn't just about authority—it was about **impact, influence, and service**.

This experience planted a seed for something that would become central to my future:

Leadership is about serving others, not just leading them.

The Power of Changing Your Circle

Through these experiences, I learned an undeniable truth:

Your environment shapes you more than you realize.

At each stage of my life, I encountered people with different mindsets:

Some were visionaries who saw beyond their struggles.
Some were stagnant, believing life would never change.
Some were mentors who offered wisdom and guidance.
Some were negative influences, always pulling others down.

I had a choice:

✓ Stay in a mindset of survival, accepting limitations.
✓ Surround myself with people who challenge me to grow.

This is a choice you have to make, too.

If the people around you are not helping you grow, it's time to find a new circle.

Reflection from Pastor Magallanes

"Joey has always been different. He didn't just do what was required—he paid attention, he learned, and he was always looking for ways to improve. Even back then, you could see that he was going to be someone who made an impact."

The Shift from Surviving to Thriving

By the time I left the **Magallanes' household**, I wasn't just another struggling student.

I had a **new mindset.**
I had a **new understanding of leadership.**
I had a **vision for something bigger.**

I was no longer just trying to get through life but preparing to create the life I wanted.

Key Lessons from Chapter 2

1. **Your environment shapes your mindset** – Choose it wisely.
2. **Growth requires stepping away from comfort and limitations** – The hardest decisions often lead to the greatest transformations.
3. **Service and leadership go hand in hand** – Helping others opens new doors for yourself.
4. **Changing your surroundings opens your mind** – Exposure to different perspectives can change your entire future.

Breaking Free: Your Turn

Every person reaches a moment when they must decide:

Will I stay in the comfort of what I know?
Or will I step into the unknown to create a better future?

This decision will shape your life more than anything else.

If you feel stuck right now, ask yourself:

Am I surrounded by people who push me to grow?
Am I holding onto a mindset that no longer serves me?
Am I willing to take risks to break free from limitations?

It is **never too late** to change your path. It is **never too late** to choose a different life.

Because **you are not stuck—you just need a new mindset.**

So, what will you choose?

Chapter 3

When Dreams Almost End

"If you can't fly then run, if you can't run then walk, if you can't walk then crawl, but whatever you do, you have to keep moving forward."
– Martin Luther King Jr.

A Reflection on Perseverance

Life is a journey, and progress isn't always fast. The important thing is to keep moving forward, no matter how small the steps. Consistency leads to success; sometimes, what feels like an ending is just a turning point.

The Test of Resilience

"Life will test you. The question is: Will you give up or fight for what you want?"

There are moments in life when everything seems to fall into place—only to be ripped away instantly. I worked hard, sacrificed, and did everything right, and for a while, it felt like my future was finally secure. Then, in a single conversation, it all fell apart.

The Dream That Was Almost Taken Away

I had made it to **seminary school**.

For years, I had fought to stay in school—moving from one household to another, working in exchange for education, and seizing every opportunity that came my way. Finally, I was in an environment that felt **right**. I was learning. I was growing.

I was building a future that I believed was meant for me. But then, one day, my **father** sat me down. His face was tired, his voice heavy.

"Son, we can't afford your education anymore."

His words felt like a punch to the gut. I tried to argue and defend my case. I tried to explain why education mattered, why I couldn't stop now. But deep inside, I knew the truth—our family **could no longer afford my studies**. And just like that, my dream of finishing seminary was over.

I felt like a failure. I had done everything right. I had worked so hard. **Was it all for nothing?** Would all my sacrifices **end in vain**? For the first time in my life, I felt **completely lost**.

The Hustle: Surviving as a Student

I had a choice.

✓ I could accept this as the end of my journey. I could go back home, work whatever job I could find, and live a **life of struggle** like so many others before me.

✓ Or I could **fight for a way forward**.

I had spent my entire life believing that if you wanted something **bad enough**, you had to find a way. So, instead of giving up, I **created another path**.

Making Ends Meet

While studying, I learned to balance **education with survival**.

With one hand, I carried my notebook, symbolizing my dreams. With the other, I carried food to sell, symbolizing my determination.

I partnered with **Tito Kapid**, our neighbor, who made **delicacies and rice cakes**. I sold them to classmates and teachers. But that wasn't enough. After school, I would go to **Banago to buy fish** and resell them when I got home. It became my daily rhythm: Study, Sell, Repeat. I also worked on a sugarcane plantation and even at a construction site—whatever I could put my hands on.

At first, I was **embarrassed**. But then, I realized something **powerful**:

There's no shame in hard work.

There's honor in doing what it takes to move forward.

Instead of **hiding my situation**, I **owned it**. I became a **role model** for other students, proving that perseverance and determination could **break barriers**. But still, the question remained—**what was next for me?**

The Crossroads: Sink or Fight?

Then I heard about **Mayor Gerry Rojas's Scholarship Program**. It was a **vocational training initiative** that provided financial support for students who couldn't afford further education. The program covered:

✓ Tuition fees
✓ Allowances
✓ Transportation costs

It wasn't **seminary school**.
It wasn't **the path I had envisioned for myself**.
But it was **something**.

And at that time, **something was enough**.

From Setback to Success

I applied for the **scholarship**, pushed through my disappointment, and **focused on what was ahead**. I enrolled in **Building and House**

Wiring—a course I had **never imagined** taking. At first, I felt **lost**. This wasn't the path I had planned. But then it hit me:

When life gives you a different opportunity than expected, don't resist it—master it.

So I did. I didn't just **attend classes**—I **excelled**. I pushed myself harder than ever before. I studied, practiced, and committed myself to **learning everything** about the trade.

And when the final exams came, something incredible happened:

I ranked top of my class.
I passed with flying colors.

What felt like a **detour** turned into a **stepping stone**. I had proved to myself that **failure is only final if you stop trying**.

A Message from Mayor Gerry Rojas

"Joey was one of the most determined students we had. He didn't just take what was given—he turned it into an opportunity to grow. That's the mindset of a leader."

The Lesson: Your Plans Can Change—And That's Okay

I never became the **pastor** I once dreamed of becoming. My life took an **entirely different path**.

But looking back, I can see clearly now that:

✓ **Life doesn't always give you what you want, but it gives you what you need.**
✓ **Success is not about sticking to one plan but adapting to new opportunities.**
✓ **Every setback carries the seed of a bigger success—if you're willing to see it.**

That moment—the moment I thought my dreams had **ended**—was actually the moment that **set me on the path to where I am today**. It was the beginning of a **mindset shift** that would guide me through even **greater challenges ahead**.

Because **life is not about what happens to you—it's about what you do with it.**

And I was just getting started.

Key Lessons from Chapter 3

1. **Failure is feedback, not final.** – Every setback teaches you something valuable.
2. **Success is not about avoiding struggles—it's about learning from them.** – Challenges shape resilience.
3. **Your ability to pivot and adapt determines your growth.** – When plans fall apart, new opportunities arise.
4. **Even when doors close, new paths can still lead to great success.** – Stay open to unexpected possibilities.

Your Turning Point

Maybe **you** are facing a moment where it feels like everything is falling apart. Maybe you feel **stuck, lost, or uncertain** about your future.

Here's what I want you to know:

Your journey is not over.
Your struggles are preparing you for something bigger.
You have the power to turn any setback into a stepping stone.

The **real question** is:

Will you give up? Or will you fight for the life you deserve?

The choice is yours!

Chapter 4

The Guiding Light – My Sister, My Rock

"A sister is both your mirror – and your opposite." – Elizabeth Fishel

A Reflection on Sibling Bonds

Siblings shape our lives in profound ways. They reflect our strengths and weaknesses, offering both comfort and challenge. Some siblings grow apart, living their own separate lives, while others become a constant presence, an unshakable foundation.

For me, my sister **Novelyn** was not just family—she was my **guiding light**. She was my **protector**, my **mentor**, my **second mother**, and my **greatest supporter**. Without her, I would not be standing where I am today.

The One Who Led the Way

Novelyn was the **first in our family** to leave home, venturing far beyond our small town to the bustling capital of the Philippines—**Manila**. She started as a **house helper**, working tirelessly in an unfamiliar city. I can only imagine how difficult it must have been for her—alone, adjusting to a new life away from the comforts of home. But she never once complained. Instead, **she lifted us up**.

She **sent money home**, ensuring we had food to eat and clothes to wear.

She **helped pay for our school uniforms**, giving us a chance at a better future.

She **became our provider**, even when she barely had enough for herself.

I was always grateful for her, but I didn't fully understand the depth of her sacrifices until much later. Even **our mother confided in her**, sharing worries and burdens she didn't reveal to anyone else.

She wasn't just helping us survive—**she was building a future for us.**

She was a **dreamer**, just like me. But unlike many, she **didn't dream for herself alone—she dreamed for our entire family**.

The Sister Who Changed My Path

Novelyn didn't just send money—**she encouraged me to dream bigger**. One day, she **convinced me to move to Manila**, just like she had. At first, I refused. I had seen others go to the city and come back **changed**—their skin fairer, their attitudes prouder. I didn't want to lose myself in a place that felt so different from home. But my sister knew exactly how to persuade me.

"Joey, you'll ride an airplane coming here," she said, making my eyes widen with excitement.

Then she added something even more enticing: **"I'll send you to the school where Sarah Geronimo studied."**

At that time, **Sarah Geronimo** was a rising star in the Star for a Night singing competition.

Now, let me tell you something about myself—I wasn't the most talented, but I had the **heart of a competitor**. During high school, I joined **every contest** that offered a prize—singing, dancing, running, poetry. If there were **money or rice to be won**, I was in. So when my sister dangled the promise of a chance to **compete and become a champion**, how could I resist?

And that was how my **journey to a bigger world began**.

My sister brought me from Manila to Qatar in 2009 and then to the **UAE in 2015**. With every step forward, **she was there, guiding me, believing in me, and showing me what was possible.**

The One Who Never Gave Up on Me

Our mother passed away in **2004**, followed by our father in **2010**. Losing both parents was a pain that never truly faded, and for a time, I felt **lost**. But Novelyn **never let me fall**. She stepped in—not just as a sister, but as **the one person who refused to let me give up**. She **took care of me, provided for me**, and ensured I had **opportunities to work, learn, and grow.**

Even when I struggled…
Even when I made mistakes…
Even when I doubted myself…

She never turned her back on me.

How many people in this world can say they have **someone like that** in their lives?

But she didn't just do this **for me**.

She did it for **all of us—her siblings**.

The Sister Who Held Us All Together

Novelyn was not just **my rock**—she was the **pillar that held our entire family together.**

As **8 siblings**, we each had our own struggles and burdens.

But she was the one who made sure:

✓ We had **food to eat.**
✓ We had **a place to sleep.**
✓ We had **a reason to keep going.**

Novelyn became **our mother and father** after our parents had gone. She carried responsibilities that no one asked of her and never **complained.** There must have been days when she was **exhausted** and when the weight of everything was **too much to bear.** But she **never showed it.** She carried it all—**without expecting anything in return.** If there is **one person** in this world who has shown me that life is more than just survival, **it is her.**

She made me believe that I could:

✓ Dream **bigger**
✓ Achieve **more**
✓ Break **free from limitations**

And because of her…
I did.

Novelyn's Words

"Joey has tremendous strength. He has unshakable faith. But I knew he needed guidance. I didn't want him to settle for something less when I knew he could do something greater. I'm proud of who he has become."

The Moment I Knew I Had to Succeed

At some point, I realized that **everything I did was no longer just for me—it was for her, too.** I had to **prove that her sacrifices were not in vain.** I had to **become someone worthy of the trust and faith she placed in me.**

So I worked **harder**.

I took **risks**.

I fought for a **future where I could finally say:**

"Ate, you don't have to worry anymore. I made it."

Everything I do—from **business to leadership**, from **personal growth to mentoring others**—is a **tribute to her sacrifices**. She gave me a **future**. And now, I dedicate my **success** to **honoring her**.

The Lesson: We All Have Someone Who Believes in Us

Take a moment to reflect—**who has been your guiding light?** Maybe it's a **family member, a mentor, or a friend** who stood by you when no one else did. Success is **never achieved alone. There is always someone who has played a role in your journey.** The **best way** to repay them is to make the **most** of the opportunities they give you. For me, that person is my sister **Novelyn**.

And if you have **someone like that in your life**—take a moment to **thank them**.

Because without them, **you might not be where you are today**.

Key Lessons from Chapter 4

1. **Having the right support system can change everything.** – The people who believe in you can shape your future.
2. **Sacrifices made for others create a lasting impact.** – One person's love and effort can uplift an entire family.
3. **Success is not a solo journey. Express gratitude for those who lifted you.** – No one succeeds alone; always acknowledge your roots.
4. **Your best mentors may come from your own family.** – Sometimes, the greatest wisdom comes from the ones who have always been there.

Who Is Your Rock?

We all have **someone** who helped shape who we are today.

Who is **your guiding light?**

Who has **sacrificed for you?**

Who has **believed in you, even when you doubted yourself?**

Success is not just about achieving personal goals—it's about **honoring those who helped us get there.** If you have someone like **Novelyn** in your life, don't wait. **Tell them. Thank them. Show them their sacrifices mattered.**

Chapter 5

The Gold Scheme in Qatar – A Costly Lesson in Resilience

"Do not be embarrassed by your failures; learn from them and start again." – Richard Branson

Reflection:

Failure is not the end—it is a stepping stone toward success. Every mistake is a lesson, and every setback is an opportunity to grow stronger and wiser. Instead of being embarrassed by our failures, we should embrace them, learn from them, and use them as fuel to start again. The most successful people in the world have faced failure, but what sets them apart is their resilience and willingness to keep moving forward. Richard Branson reminds us that success is built on the courage to rise after falling.

One of the hardest lessons for me came in **2014, in Qatar**, when I found myself trapped in a **gold scheme scam** that nearly destroyed everything I had worked for.

This chapter is not just about a mistake—it's about **betrayal, survival, and the painful cost of trust.** But most importantly, it's about **rising from the ashes** and proving that **failure is never the finish line.**

The Promise of Wealth

It all started with an **opportunity**.

At that time, I had **built a good career in Qatar**. I was surrounded by ambitious people, many of whom were also looking for ways to grow their wealth.

Then, someone approached me with an **investment proposal**—a gold trading business. The offer seemed **legitimate**. The person behind it was someone I trusted, someone who had already gained **credibility within the Filipino community in Qatar**.

The deal was simple:

✓ **Invest money**
✓ **Help bring in more investors**
✓ **Receive high monthly returns**

It **seemed like the perfect way** to multiply my income. Many others were already involved, and they were **seeing results**. I did my **research**. I asked **questions**. Everything appeared **legal and secure**. So, I took the risk.

The Illusion of Success

At first, the **returns came exactly as promised**.

Money was flowing.
Everything seemed to be going as planned.
I was confident this was my **big break into financial freedom**.

But then, things started to **change**.

The Moment Everything Collapsed

One day, the **returns stopped coming**. I reached out to the **people running the investment**, but the responses became **vague**.

Promises turned into delays.

Delays turned into silence.

Then, the truth came out.

The entire operation was a **scam**.

The money was gone.

The people behind it disappeared.

And those of us who invested? We were left with nothing but regret.

I **didn't just lose money**—I lost my **reputation**.

I lost the **trust** of people who had followed me into this investment.

I lost my **sense of security** in a country that was not my own.

In an instant, **everything crumbled**.

Sharing the Same Pain – I Was a Victim Too

I wasn't the **mastermind**.

I wasn't even in **control** of the business.

I was just **another victim**.

I had **invested just like everyone else**. I had put my **hard-earned money** into something I believed was legitimate. But when the scam was exposed, people **didn't care** about that—they just **wanted their money back**. Some people **blamed me** simply because I had **shared the opportunity** with them. They didn't understand that **I was suffering the loss too**.

I had lost everything. And yet, despite being a victim myself, I chose not to succumb to a victim mindset. Instead of **running away**, I did what I could to **help**. I managed to **pay back some of the people** who had lost money, even though it was not **my sole responsibility**. **I didn't have all the money to pay everyone back, but I gave what I could.**

Because I **knew what it felt like** to lose everything.

Running for Survival

The situation **escalated quickly**.

! People were **angry**.
! They **wanted answers**.
! Some of them **blamed me** because I had believed in the business and encouraged others to invest.

The **worst part of it?** I, too, was a victim. But **no one wanted to hear that**. I wasn't just **fighting for my financial survival**—I was also **fighting to clear my name**. But in Qatar, financial disputes can **lead to serious legal trouble**. So, I **knew I had to leave**.

Finding Light in the Dark

With a **heavy heart**, I fled to **Nepal**. I didn't know what was **waiting for me** there. All I knew was that I needed to:
Escape
Find a way to survive
Figure out how to rebuild my life

This was when I **hit rock bottom**.

The Three Lessons That Saved Me

Sitting alone **outside the house of my best friend Divash in Manahari, Nepal**, I had a choice:

✗ Drown in regret and self-pity
✓ Rise from the mess I was in and start again

I remembered **everything I had gone through before**—the struggles, the sacrifices, the people who believed in me.

I couldn't let **this be the end of my story.**

I turned to my **faith.**

I **prayed.**

I **reflected.**

I realized that **this failure does not define me.**

I made a decision:

I will rebuild myself.
I will rise again.

Because **life is not about never falling—it's about getting up every single time you do.**

Returning With a New Mindset

I **made a decision.** I wasn't going to let this **failure be the end** of my story. In **2015**, I moved to **the UAE.** I had to **start from scratch.**

But this time, I had a **new mindset:**

✔ **I would be more cautious about business opportunities.**
✔ **I would build multiple sources of income.**
✔ **I would rise—not just for myself, but for those who believed in me.**

I was **no longer just surviving.**
I was **preparing to thrive.**

A New Beginning

Failure did not break me—it built me. I took what I **learned** and turned it into **fuel for my next chapter.** I used my experience to:

Educate others about financial literacy.

Warn people about the dangers of scams.
Mentor aspiring entrepreneurs.

And most importantly, I made a **vow:**

No scam, deception, or betrayal would ever take away my future again.

The past was a **painful lesson**. But the future? **That was mine to create.** And so, **I did.**

Key Lessons from Chapter 5

1. **Trust must be earned, not assumed.** – Never blindly trust an opportunity, no matter how promising it seems.
2. **Financial education is crucial.** – Always understand what you're investing in before taking risks.
3. **Setbacks are temporary, but resilience lasts forever.** – What seems like the end is often just a new beginning.
4. **Integrity is more valuable than money.** – How you handle failure defines you more than your successes.

Your Next Step

Maybe **you** have faced a failure that shook your confidence.
Maybe **you** have been betrayed by people you trusted.
Maybe **you** feel like **giving up**.

But let me tell you this:

Your failure does not define you.
You can rebuild.
You can rise again.

The real question is:

Will you let failure break you or use it to build something greater?

The choice is **yours**.

Chapter 6

From Survival to Strategy – The CEO Mindset

"The way to get started is to quit talking and begin doing." – Walt Disney

A Reflection on Execution and Action

Too often, people stay stuck in **planning mode**. They wait for the **right moment, the right opportunity, and the perfect conditions**. But the truth is that **success belongs to those who act**.

The **CEO mindset** is about execution. It's about taking charge, making decisions, and moving forward—even when the path isn't clear. **Dreams remain dreams unless we act on them.**

"Surviving is not enough. To truly succeed, you must start thinking like a CEO—of your life, your career, and your future."

After experiencing one of the **lowest points in my life**, I made a decision:

☑ **I would no longer just survive.**
☑ **I would start building strategically.**

The **gold scheme scam** in Qatar had **taught me painful but necessary lessons:**

✓ **Trust wisely**
✓ **Invest smartly**

✓ **Always have multiple streams of income**

When I returned to the **UAE in 2015**, I was **not the same person** I once was. I had a **new mindset** and a **new purpose**.

This chapter is about how I transformed from someone **simply trying to recover**—to someone **ready to rebuild and take control** of my life.

The Turning Point: Choosing to Take Control

For years, my life had been about **reacting to circumstances**:

I worked hard, but I had **no financial strategy**.
I grabbed opportunities, but I **didn't always do due diligence**.
I survived failures but **wasn't building a system to protect myself** from future risks.

And then, I realized something **powerful**:

If I wanted lasting success, I needed to think like a CEO—not just an employee or an entrepreneur, but the CEO of my own life.

What Does It Mean to Think Like a CEO?

A **CEO** doesn't just **work hard** but **builds systems** that ensure **long-term success**.
A **CEO** doesn't **rely on just one source of income** but **diversifies** and creates **financial security**.
A **CEO** doesn't **avoid failure** but **learns from failure** and turns it into an **advantage**.

So, I asked myself:

What can I build that no one can take away from me?

Step 1: Diversifying My Income Streams

One of the **biggest lessons** I learned after the **Qatar gold scheme failure** was:

Never put all your money in one place.

I started looking at **different ways** to generate income and **protect my financial future**:

✅ **Coaching and Consulting** – I began conducting **workshops and training programs** focused on **personal development, sales, marketing, and business strategies.**
✅ **Embracing Passive Income** – Instead of just selling **one thing**, I invested in **financial literacy, AI-driven opportunities, and wellness products** that **generate income over time.**
✅ **Mastering Digital Marketing** – I leveraged **WhatsApp marketing, social media, and online branding** to **attract clients instead of chasing them.**

The Result?

✓ I was **no longer dependent** on just **one source of income.**
✓ I was **building a portfolio** of businesses and investments that could **sustain me long-term.**

Step 2: Shifting from Hard Work to Smart Work

I used to believe that **working harder** was the key to success.

But I realized:

✗ **Working harder is NOT enough.**
✅ **Smart work beats hard work.**

It's **not about working more hours**—it's about **working on the right things.**

Instead of just **selling**, I focused on **building a brand** that **attracts clients**.

Instead of **doing everything alone**, I **built a network** of people who could grow with me.

Instead of just **making money**, I focused on **creating systems** that generate income **even when I'm not working**.

Step 3: Leadership and Mentorship – Creating Impact

I also realized that **true success** isn't just about **money**—it's about the **impact you create**. That's why I became more involved in:

✓ **Toastmasters and Public Speaking** – Refining my **communication skills** to become a **better leader**.
✓ **Mentorship** – Helping others **navigate their own journeys** by turning my **failures into lessons** for them.
✓ **Coaching** – Guiding people toward **financial literacy** and **career growth**.

Why?

Because **success feels different** when it's **not just about you** but about **lifting others as you rise**.

The Power of Lifelong Learning: Unlocking Growth Through Mindset and Exploration

Growth is **not automatic**—it is a **choice**.

The **key to success** lies in our ability to **keep learning** and **exploring new things**.

Why Continuous Learning is Crucial

It keeps you adaptable – The world is constantly changing. Those who keep learning **stay ahead**.

It opens new opportunities – Learning new skills can lead to **career shifts, business ventures, or life-changing discoveries**.
It strengthens mental agility – The brain thrives on **new challenges, problem-solving, and innovation**.
It builds confidence – Knowledge **increases self-worth and resilience**.
It expands your network – Learning **connects you** to new people, mentors, and communities.

Developing a Lifelong Learning Attitude

✓ **Stay Curious** – Ask questions, read books, and **challenge your beliefs**.

✓ **Step Out of Your Comfort Zone** – Growth happens when you **try something new**.

✓ **Learn from Failures** – Every mistake is an **expensive lesson—use it wisely**.

✓ **Surround Yourself with Growth-Oriented People** – You become **who you spend time with**.

✓ **Make Learning a Daily Habit** – **Read, take courses, attend seminars—never stop learning**.

The moment you stop exploring, you stop growing.

I want to express my deepest gratitude to the people who continuously inspire me to keep learning and growing.

To my dearest **Desert Voices Toastmasters Club that belongs to Area 7, Division B of District 127,** and the entire **Toastmasters community**—your support, encouragement, and dedication to communication and leadership excellence have been invaluable in my journey.

To my **Mastermind Learners—Sir Rolly Brucales, Norvin Apat, Jewel Arevalo, Charry Dela Cruz, Charisma Abelardo, and Cristina**

Manalo—thank you for the shared wisdom, collaboration, and commitment to lifelong learning.

I would like to give a special acknowledgment to our **mentor and coach, Michelle Tatel**, whose guidance and insights have been instrumental in our continuous growth.

Above all, all **glory and honor belong to Jesus Christ alone,** my greatest source of **strength and wisdom.**

The CEO Mindset: Key Lessons

✓ **Never depend on one income stream.** Always have **multiple sources of income.**
✓ **Work smarter, not just harder.** Build **systems, not just schedules.**
✓ **Build your personal brand.** Your **network and reputation matter more** than any job.
✓ **Learn to lead.** Leadership is about **creating opportunities for others, not just yourself.**
✓ **Turn your failures into wisdom.** Every mistake is an **expensive lesson—use it wisely.**

The Moment Everything Changed

✓ I stopped **living paycheck to paycheck.**
✓ I stopped **reacting to life** and started **creating opportunities.**
✓ I stopped **seeing failure as the end**—and started **using it as fuel for growth.**

✅ That is when everything changed.
✅ That is when I stopped **just surviving**—and started **building.**

Key Lessons from Chapter 6

✅ **Never depend on one income stream—diversification is the key.**
✅ **Work smarter, not just harder—systems create success.**

✓ **Building a personal brand attracts opportunities.**
✓ **True leadership is about impact, not just personal gain.**

Your Future is in Your Hands

What system are you building today that will secure your tomorrow?
What skills are you learning that will open new doors?
What steps are you taking today to create financial and personal freedom?

The truth is—**you are already the CEO of your life.**

It's time to start acting like one.

Chapter 7

Love, Faith, and The Power of Community

"Alone, we can do so little; together, we can do so much." – Helen Keller

A Reflection on the Strength of Relationships

Success is rarely achieved alone. We may have talent, ambition, and drive, but without the right people supporting us, our journey can feel empty and unsustainable.

Faith and community provide the foundation for lasting success. They give us **strength when we feel weak, guidance when we feel lost**, and **encouragement when we doubt ourselves.**

Behind every strong leader is a **strong support system**. And for me, that system includes my **wife, Thirdly, our spiritual mentors, and our church community**.

Success Is Never Achieved Alone

Every breakthrough I have experienced, every moment of resilience I have displayed, and every challenge I have overcome—none of it would have been possible without the **love, support, and prayers of the people around me.**

It is easy to focus on **financial success, leadership skills, and personal growth**, but **without faith and a solid support system, success can feel empty**.

No matter how strong or capable we are, **we all need people who believe in us, guide us, and walk with us on this journey.**

Meeting My Greatest Blessing

In **2016**, I met the woman who would become my **biggest supporter, my encourager, and my life partner—Thirdly**. From the moment I met her at church, I knew **she was special**.

She wasn't just **kind**—she was **strong**.
She wasn't just **loving**—she was **full of faith**.

In **2017, we got married**, and my **life changed forever**. She has been with me through **every high and low, every risk and reward**.

✔ She encourages me when I **doubt myself**.
✔ She prays for me when I **face challenges**.
✔ She believes in me—even when **I struggle to believe in myself**.

There is a saying:

"Behind every successful man is a strong woman."

But **Thirdly isn't just behind me**—she is **beside me**, walking this journey with me, **hand in hand**. Her **faith and unwavering love** have given me the **strength to rise again and again**, no matter how many times life has tried to knock me down.

The Mentors Who Strengthened Our Faith

Alongside my wife, **our faith community** has played a **crucial role** in our growth—both **spiritually and in life**. In church, we found not just **friends** but **mentors**—people who **consistently guided and**

encouraged us in our **spiritual journey**. These are the people who have been with us **through thick and thin**—our **Discipleship Group (D-Group)**:

Jeffrey and Mitzie Tubay – Providing encouragement and unwavering support.

Alvin and Marivic Alfaro with Audree – Standing by us in faith and generosity.

Matthew and Aileen Ormeo with Ainah – Always offering wisdom and love.

Ronald and Beth Castillo with Kharylle – Being a source of inspiration.

Mike and Sophie Tamayo – Walking alongside us in faith and growth.

From the **beginning of our marriage**, our **D-Group leaders, Jeffrey and Mitzie, have been incredibly patient and supportive.**

They **helped us strengthen our faith.**
They **guided us through challenges.**
They **taught us the power of accountability in marriage, personal growth, and spirituality.**

Having an **accountability group** of **Christ-like individuals** has been **life-changing.**

Through them, we learned:

✓ **Faith is not just personal—it's something we build in the community.**

✓ **Success is not just financial—it's also spiritual and emotional.**

✓ **Growth happens faster when we have people who uplift and challenge us.**

And with them, our **entire church community** has been **praying for us**, **lifting us up**, and **helping us move forward with God's amazing grace**.

Why Faith and Community Matter

People often talk about **skills, strategies, and mindset** when it comes to **success in business and life**. But the **greatest foundation** for success is **faith and the right people around you**.

✓ **The right partner in life can multiply your potential.**
✓ **Having mentors and a faith-driven community will sustain you when challenges arise.**
✓ **Your success is not just about financial freedom – it's about spiritual and emotional strength, too.**

Hard work matters.

Strategy is essential.

But at the end of the day, what keeps you going is **love, faith, and community**.

A Message to You

If you are on a journey to success, **don't walk it alone**.

Find the right partner—someone who **lifts you up, prays for you, and walks with you.**
Surround yourself with good mentors—people who **have been where you want to go.**
Stay connected to a faith-driven community—because when **life gets tough**, you'll need people who will **stand by you**.

For me, **Thirdly and our church family** have been my **foundation**; because of them, I am **stronger, wiser, and more grounded** than ever before.

Key Lessons from Chapter 7

✓ **The right life partner multiplies your potential.** – Choosing a supportive and faith-driven partner can **elevate** your journey.

✓ **Faith and a strong support system sustain you in difficult times.** – When **life tests you**, the people around you **will determine how well you confront the situation.**

✓ **Surround yourself with people who uplift, inspire, and hold you accountable.** – You **become like the people** you spend the most time with—**choose wisely.**

✓ **Success without community feels empty—build relationships, not just wealth.** – At the **end of the day, success is about the lives we touch.**

Final Thoughts: Who's in Your Circle?

Who are the people **supporting you** in your journey?
Do you have **mentors** who guide you spiritually and professionally?
Are you part of a **community** that lifts you up?

The people in your life **either pull you down or push you forward.**

✓ **Surround yourself with faith-driven, growth-oriented individuals.**

✓ **Find mentors who have already achieved what you aspire to.**

✓ **Invest in relationships that strengthen you, not drain you.**

Your **success is not just about what you build**—it's about **who you build it with.**

Make sure your circle is helping you grow!

Chapter 8
Creating a Legacy Beyond Wealth

"Try not to become a man of success, but rather try to become a man of value." – Albert Einstein

A Reflection on Legacy and Impact

Success is fleeting, but the impact is lasting. Wealth may come and go, but the **value we create, the knowledge we share, and the people we uplift**—those things last forever. At some point in life, **you realize that money alone isn't enough.**

Yes, **financial security is important.**
Yes, **building businesses and investments matter.**

But the real question is:

✓ **What impact am I making?**
✓ **Who am I helping?**
✓ **What will I leave behind?**

The Shift From Success to Significance

For years, I focused on **rebuilding my life**. I learned how to:

Earn wisely.
Invest strategically.
Grow multiple businesses.

But **something was missing. True success isn't about how much you make but how many lives you touch.** So I started asking myself:

✓ **Who am I helping along the way?**
✓ **How am I using my story to inspire others?**
✓ **Am I lifting people up just as others lifted me?**

That's when I realized:

My legacy will not be measured by my bank account.
It will be measured by the lives I impact.

Empowering Others Through Training and Workshops

One of the most powerful ways to create a legacy is through **education**—not just traditional degrees but **real-world knowledge that changes lives**. That's why I became deeply involved in **workshops and training programs** that focus on:

✓ **Personal Development and Leadership** – Helping individuals **discover their potential** and **build confidence.**
✓ **Financial Literacy and Wealth Building** – Teaching people **how to manage money, invest, and create financial freedom.**
✓ **Business and Entrepreneurship** – Equipping aspiring entrepreneurs with **the skills to start and grow businesses.**
✓ **Sales & Marketing Strategies** – Showing professionals **how to leverage branding, social media, and digital marketing to scale their income.**

Why?

Because **I know the challenge of finding the right guidance.** I know what it's like **to feel lost, to lack direction, to not know where to start.** That's why I made it my **mission** to help others **find clarity and confidence.**

Knowledge is the one thing no one can take away from you. And when you **share knowledge**, you **multiply its power.** That's a legacy worth building.

Your Legacy is Not Just About You

What I've learned on this journey is this:

✓ **Success is about YOU, but a legacy is about OTHERS.**

If your only goal is **to get rich,** your **impact will die with you.** But if your goal is to **change lives, empower people, and create opportunities**—your **legacy will live on forever.**

I don't want to **just be remembered as someone who made money. I want to be remembered as someone who made a difference.**

Because at the end of the day:

The real measure of success is not what you gain but what you give.

Giving Back: The True Measure of Wealth

True **financial freedom** is not just about **having money**—it's about **using it wisely.** For me, that means:

✓ **Helping young entrepreneurs start businesses.**
✓ **Teaching financial literacy to those who never learned it.**
✓ **Sponsoring education and mentorship programs for aspiring leaders.**
✓ **Investing in communities that need opportunities.**

When we **give back,** we don't just **help others**—we **multiply our own success.**

Why?

✓ Because **when you empower others, you create opportunities for yourself.**

✓ Because **wealth should be a tool for change, not just personal comfort.**

✓ Because **true success is measured by the impact you leave behind.**

The Three Pillars of a Meaningful Legacy

1. Teaching Others

Knowledge is power—but only if it is shared.

Every lesson I have learned, every failure I have faced, every breakthrough I have experienced—I see all of it as something **meant to be shared with others.**

✓ **If I teach one person how to build wealth, they can teach another.**
✓ **If I mentor one entrepreneur, they can inspire many more.**

Legacy isn't just about **what you do**—it's about **what you pass on.**

2. Creating Sustainable Wealth

Wealth that **only benefits you** is **temporary.**

Wealth that is **built wisely** and **invested in others** is **everlasting.**

That's why I focus on **smart investing** and **multiple income streams**, not just for myself but also to **teach others how to do the same.**

Passive income allows you to create freedom—not just for yourself, but for others. Smart investments ensure that wealth outlives you. Teaching financial literacy helps people break generational cycles of poverty.

A true legacy isn't just money – it's financial wisdom that lasts for generations.

3. Lifting Others as You Rise

Someone once told me:

"The best way to measure success is by counting the people you've helped."

I **carry that truth with me** in everything I do.

That's why my focus is on:

✓ **Mentorship programs**
✓ **Leadership development**
✓ **Supporting small businesses**
✓ **Creating a network of success-minded individuals**

Because **when we lift others up, we all rise together. A true legacy is not about personal success but collective growth.**

Success vs. Legacy: The Real Difference

Success is about YOU.
Legacy is about OTHERS.

Success is about how much you make.
Legacy is about how much you give.

Success is about personal achievement.
Legacy is about how you inspire and empower others.

At the end of the day, **what matters most is not what you have—it's what you leave behind.**

Key Lessons from Chapter 8

✓ **Success is about impact, not just income.** – The best measure of wealth is **how many lives you change**.
✓ **Teaching others is the most powerful way to leave a lasting legacy.** – Knowledge **multiplies** when shared.

✓ **True financial freedom comes from smart investing and passive income.** – Wealth should be built to **outlive you**.

✓ **Your legacy is defined by how many lives you have changed.** – Your **true success** is measured by the **impact you make**.

A Final Thought on Your Legacy

What are you building today that will still matter in 10, 20, or 50 years?

How are you **using your success to empower others**?

What knowledge, lessons, or resources can you share to **create opportunities for someone else**?

Your success is temporary. Your impact is forever.

So start today.

Build wisely.
Teach generously.
Lift others up.

Because **your real legacy is not what you leave behind; it's who you help along the way.**

Chapter 9

The Leadership Philosophy That Changed My Life

"Leadership is not about being in charge. It is about taking care of those in your charge." – Simon Sinek

A Reflection on True Leadership

Leadership isn't about **authority**—it's about **responsibility**. A great leader isn't someone who simply gives orders; a great leader is someone who **inspires, empowers, and serves others**. When I look back at my journey—from **struggling to surviving, from surviving to thriving**—I realize one powerful truth:

Leadership is not about a title.

It's about influence, service, and the ability to create change.

For years, I **chased success**, believing leadership was about **power and authority**.

But the more I grew, the more I saw that **true leadership is about lifting others as you rise.**

The Beginning of My Leadership Journey

My leadership journey started in **college** when I became **President of Student Affairs** in my second year. That role **changed my perspective**. It wasn't just about:

✓ Leading meetings
✓ Making decisions
✓ Holding a title

It was about:

✓ **Empowering others**
✓ **Creating opportunities for people to grow**
✓ **Serving a bigger purpose**

The Defining Experience That Shaped My Leadership Mindset

One of the most defining experiences of my life came in **2007** when I was selected to represent my school in **India** for an **interfaith dialog program**. I spent over **3 months at the School of Peace**, engaging with people from **20 conflict-affected countries**.

We had **deep conversations about religion, culture, and leadership**. We discussed **how to promote peace and harmony in divided communities**.
We **listened, learned, and sought solutions that went beyond personal gain**.

This experience **shaped my leadership philosophy forever**.

✓ Leadership is **not about status**—it's about **responsibility**.
✓ Leadership is **not about what you gain** but **what you give**.
✓ Leadership is **not about control**—it's about **service**.

That was the moment I knew:

I didn't want to be a leader just for personal success.
I wanted to be a leader who made a lasting impact.

The Leadership Principles That Changed My Life

Here are the key leadership lessons that transformed not only my business and career but also my **purpose and the people around me.**

1. Lead Yourself First

Leadership starts from within.

Before you can lead others, you must first **master yourself.**

Self-discipline – Control your habits and emotions.
Self-awareness – Understand your strengths and weaknesses.
Self-improvement – Constantly learn and evolve.

There were moments in my journey when I **lacked clarity** and made **fear-based decisions** instead of **vision-driven ones.** But everything changed when I started investing in my personal growth—reading, training, and surrounding myself with the right mentors.

Lesson: Don't expect to lead others if you can't lead yourself.

2. Leadership is About Service or Status

For years, I thought leadership was about **power and success.** But I realized:

Leadership is not about being in charge but about serving others.

That's why I became passionate about:

✓ **Mentoring entrepreneurs and professionals**
✓ **Guiding people in financial literacy and wealth-building**
✓ **Helping aspiring leaders find their voice through Toastmasters and coaching**

Leadership is not a position; it's a mission.

Lesson: If your leadership is only about you, you're doing it wrong.

3. Communicate with Clarity and Purpose

A great leader is **not the one who knows everything** but the one who can **communicate effectively.**

Through **Toastmasters International**, I learned how to:

☑ **Speak with confidence and impact**
☑ **Motivate teams and inspire action**
☑ **Share my story in a way that resonates with others**

Lesson: Your success in leadership depends on how well you communicate your vision.

4. Take Risks and Embrace Failure

Great leaders are not afraid to take risks.

One of my **biggest failures**—the **gold scheme in Qatar**—was painful.

But it taught me to be:

✓ **Smarter**
✓ **More strategic**
✓ **More resilient**

Instead of letting **failure define me,** I let it **refine me. The best leaders fail fast and learn fast.**

Lesson: Failure is part of leadership. But so is learning, adapting, and growing stronger.

5. Surround Yourself with the Right People

You cannot lead alone. Many people **try to do everything themselves** and **fail**. The greatest leaders build **strong networks**. They surround themselves with:

✓ **Mentors who guide them**
✓ **Peers who challenge them**
✓ **Teams that support them**

That's why I invested in **building relationships—**

✓ Through **Toastmasters**
✓ Through **business communities**
✓ Through **leadership networks**

Lesson: If you want to grow as a leader, grow your network.

6. Be the Leader You Wish You Had

I've had **amazing mentors**. But I've also experienced moments of **feeling lost and alone**. So I made a promise:

I will be the leader I once needed.

✓ **A leader who gives opportunities to others**
✓ **A leader who shares knowledge instead of keeping it**
✓ **A leader who leads with integrity and purpose**

Lesson: Leadership is not about being the boss but about being an example.

7. Leadership is About Legacy

At the end of the day, leadership is not just about success.

✓ It's about **creating something that lasts beyond you.**
✓ It's about **mentoring the next generation of leaders.**

✓ It's about **ensuring your impact continues long after you've gone**.

That's why **legacy-driven leadership is my mission**.

Because when you **focus on serving, inspiring, and empowering others—**

You don't just become successful; you become unforgettable.

Lesson: The best leaders don't just build businesses. They build people.

Final Thoughts: Leadership is a Journey

Leadership isn't something you achieve; something you practice every day.

I am **still learning**.
I am **still growing**.

Every **challenge, every failure, every success** teaches me how to **be better**.

So, if you want to be a leader, remember this:

✓ **Lead yourself first.**
✓ **Focus on service, not status.**
✓ **Communicate with clarity.**
✓ **Take risks and embrace failure.**
✓ **Surround yourself with the right people.**
✓ **Be the leader you wish you had.**
✓ **Think beyond success—think legacy.**

Because the world doesn't need **more successful people. It needs more leaders who create impact.** And that is the kind of leader **I strive to be**.

Key Lessons from Chapter 9

☑ **Lead yourself first** – Self-discipline is the foundation of success.

☑ **Great leaders serve others, not just themselves.**

☑ **Communication is key** – Your vision is only as strong as your ability to express it.

☑ **Your network determines your net worth** – Surround yourself with the right people.

☑ **Leadership is about legacy** – The best leaders build people, not just businesses.

Will you lead with purpose or just chase success? The choice is yours.

Chapter 10

Be the CEO of Your Life

"Whether you think you can, or you think you can't – you're right." – Henry Ford

A Reflection on Mindset and Leadership

Our **mindset** determines our **reality**. You will if you believe in your ability to lead and create success. If you **believe you are powerless**, you will **stay stuck**.

The truth is:

Your life is your business – manage it like a CEO.

Throughout my journey, I've learned something crucial:

☑ **You are responsible for your own success.**
☑ **You are responsible for your own failures.**
☑ **You are responsible for your own growth.**

For too long, I believed that **life just happened to me**—that my **circumstances dictated my future**. But the moment I started **thinking like a CEO, everything changed**.

This chapter is about **taking full ownership of your life** by:

✓ Making **intentional choices**
✓ Managing your **time and energy like a business**
✓ Designing a **future that excites you**

Because if **companies need CEOs to succeed**, why shouldn't **YOU** act like the **CEO of your own life?**

The CEO Mindset: Take Ownership of Everything

What is that one thing all **great CEOs** have in common?

They don't make excuses. They take ownership.

If something isn't working, **they fix it.**
If they lack skills, **they learn.**
If they fail, **they analyse and adapt.**

That's **exactly** how you need to approach life.

✓ **If your finances are struggling**—don't blame the economy. Learn **financial literacy.**
✓ **If your career is stagnant**—don't wait for a promotion. **Create opportunities.**
✓ **If your health is declining**—don't blame your schedule. **Prioritize wellness.**

A CEO doesn't wait for things to change. A CEO makes things happen.

The moment you **stop blaming others** and take **full control of your life,** you will see a **massive transformation.**

Step 1: Set a Vision for Your Life

Every great company has a vision. Every great leader knows where they're going. So let me ask you:

What is YOUR vision for your life?

Not just **your career.**
Not just **your finances.**
But your **whole life.**

✓ **Where do you want to be in 5 years?**
✓ **What kind of relationships do you want to have?**
✓ **What impact do you want to create?**

Write it down. Be clear.

Because without a vision, you will drift.

Step 2: Build Systems, Not Just Goals

Most people **set goals**, but **successful people**?

They build systems that make success inevitable.

For example:

✗ **Goal:** "I want to be financially free."
✓ **System:** "I will save 20% of my income, invest in real estate, and create passive income streams."
✗ **Goal:** "I want to be a great speaker."
✓ **System:** "I will join Toastmasters, practice weekly, and speak at events."

Goals give direction. Systems create results.

If you're serious about success, **don't just dream**—build the **systems that make success automatic.**

Step 3: Protect Your Time Like a CEO

What is a CEO's most valuable asset?

Time.

You can always **make more money.**
You can never **make more time.**

That's why you must prioritize **high-value activities**:

✓ Stop **wasting time** on negativity and distractions.
✓ Invest **time in learning, networking, and execution.**
✓ **Delegate** tasks that don't serve your bigger vision.

If something doesn't move you closer to your vision, eliminate it.

Time is your currency—spend it wisely.

Step 4: Surround Yourself with Winners

The people around you directly affect your mindset and success.

Ask yourself:

✓ **Do my friends push me toward my goals or hold me back?**
✓ **Am I surrounded by people who challenge and inspire me?**
✓ **Who do I need to start spending more time with?**

Great CEOs build great teams.

If you want to **elevate your life, elevate your circle.**

✓ **Mentors** who are ahead of you.
✓ **Peers** who are ambitious and driven.
✓ **People** who challenge you to be your best.

If you want to be a CEO, you need to start thinking like one. And that starts with surrounding yourself with the right kind of people.

Step 5: Always Be Open to Learning and Adapting

The best CEOs never stop learning.

The world is **changing fast,** industries are **evolving and** markets are **shifting**. And if you **don't adapt,** you will **be left behind**. That's why **personal development is non-negotiable.**

✓ **Read books.**
✓ **Attend seminars.**
✓ **Seek mentors.**
✓ **Invest in courses.**

Your success will always be limited by what you don't know.

So the more you **learn**, the more you **earn**.

Step 6: Take Decisive Action

Here's the harsh truth: Most people don't fail because they lack knowledge. They **fail** because they don't **take action**. They **read books**, watch motivational videos, and attend seminars, but they never **execute. That's the difference between dreamers and achievers. Achievers take decisive action.**

So whatever you've learned in this book—

Start applying it TODAY.

✓ **Want to start a business?** Make the first call **today**.
✓ **Want to improve your skills?** Enroll in a course **today**.
✓ **Want to change your life?** Take the first step **today**.

Stop waiting. Start executing.

Because nothing changes until you take action.

Final Thoughts: Own Your Life Like a CEO

At the end of the day, your life is your business.

✓ **You are the CEO.**
✓ **You set the vision.**
✓ **You make the decisions.**
✓ **You determine how far you go.**

No one else will do it **for you.**

So take control.
Take ownership.
And build a life so powerful that it inspires others to do the same.

Because **you were never meant to just exist; you were meant to lead, impact, and thrive.**

What's Next? The Journey Continues…

This book is not the end but the beginning of your transformation.

Now, it's time for you to:

✓ Take everything you've learned and **put it into action.**
✓ Start making **CEO-level decisions** in your life.
✓ Create the **systems and habits** that lead to success.
✓ Surround yourself with **people who elevate you.**
✓ Keep **learning, growing, and leading**.

Remember:

You are the CEO of your life.
You have the power to create your future.
You have everything it takes to build a life of success, impact, and legacy.

So, let's go. **The world is waiting for you.**

> *"If you want something you've never had, you must be willing to do something you've never done."* – **Thomas Jefferson**

Key Lessons from Chapter 10

✓ **Take full ownership of your success—no excuses.**
✓ **Success requires vision, systems, and action.**

☑ **Time is your most valuable asset—spend it wisely.**

☑ **Start today—small, consistent actions create massive results.**

The question is: Are you willing to manage your life like a CEO?

The choice is **yours.**

Epilogue: Your Journey as a CEO Begins Now

"Your time is limited, so don't waste it living someone else's life." – Steve Jobs

A Reflection on Taking Control of Your Life

Life is too short to **live according to other people's expectations**. It's too precious to **play small, stay safe, or hold back** because of **fear, doubt, or the opinions of others**.

This is YOUR journey, YOUR future, YOUR success. You are not here just to **exist** but to **thrive, lead, and create something meaningful**.

This will require you to:

✓ **Embrace your unique journey**
✓ **Take risks that align with your purpose**
✓ **Refuse to settle for a life that doesn't excite you**

Because at the end of the day, **the greatest investment you will ever make is in yourself.**

Your Life is a Series of Choices

As I reflect on my journey—the **struggles, the failures, the victories**—I see a pattern. Every time **life knocked me down**, I had 2 choices:

Stay down and accept defeat or

Rise again and turn the challenge into an opportunity.

I always **chose to rise**.

When I faced **financial loss**, I didn't let it define me. I **rebuilt**.
When I faced **setbacks in business**, I didn't quit. I **adapted**.
When people **doubted me**, I didn't prove them right. I **proved myself right**.

And now, as you come to the **final chapter of this book**, I ask you:

What will YOU choose?

Because this is **not just a book**—it's an **invitation**.

An invitation to take ownership of your life.
An invitation to dream bigger.
An invitation to think and act like the CEO of your future.

At the end of the day, **your success is not determined by your past.**

It is determined by the decisions you make TODAY.

The CEO Mindset for Life

If there's **one thing** I hope you take away from this book, it's this:

✓ **You are capable of more than you think.**
✓ **Your struggles do not define you—your response to them does.**
✓ **Success is not about luck but strategy, systems, and action.**
✓ **Your leadership is your legacy—start building it now.**

No one is going to hand you success.
No one is going to build your dream for you.

It's up to YOU.

So, the question is:

Will you take full control of your life and act like a CEO?

If your answer is **YES**, then your journey **starts NOW**.

Your Next Steps: A Call to Action

Before you **put this book down**, I want you to do something:

Take action RIGHT NOW. Here's how:

✓ **Step 1: Write down one BIG goal** you will commit to achieving in the next **90 days**.

✓ **Step 2: Identify one action step** you will take **TODAY** to move closer to that goal.

✓ **Step 3: Find a mentor, accountability partner, or community** that will support your growth.

✓ **Step 4: Commit to lifelong learning**—read, attend workshops, invest in personal development.

Success is not a single event; it's a journey.

Every day, every choice, and every habit add up to make you successful.

So start **today**.
Start **now**.

Your future is waiting.

The Road Ahead: Challenges and Opportunities

As you embark on this journey, let me **remind you**:

It won't always be easy and there will be setbacks, failures, and moments of doubt.

But:

✓ **Every challenge is an opportunity to grow.**
✓ **Every failure is a lesson in disguise.**
✓ **Every obstacle is a test of your commitment.**

Success is reserved for those who refuse to give up.

So, as you take your **next steps**:

Stay committed.
Stay hungry.
Stay relentless.

Because **the best version of you** is waiting on the other side of **consistent effort and bold action.**

A Thank You

To those who have walked this journey with me, supported me, and believed in me—even when I doubted myself—THANK YOU.

To those who apply the lessons from this book to their lives—**I CELEBRATE YOU.**

And to YOU, reading this now, I leave you with this:

Be bold.
Be relentless.
Be the leader you were meant to be.

Because success is **not just about what you achieve**—it's about **what you leave behind.**

Final Words: It's Time to Build Your Legacy

At the end of your life, **what will truly matter?**

✘ It won't be the **money you made**.

✘ It won't be the **titles you held**.

✘ It won't be the **cars, houses, or material things you owned**.

What will matter is the impact you created.

Did you inspire others to believe in themselves?
Did you empower people to chase their dreams?
Did you use your success to lift others up?

Because **legacy is not about wealth**—it's about **significance**.

So:

✓ **Build a life that matters.**
✓ **Create a future that excites you.**
✓ **Lead with courage, vision, and integrity.**

The world doesn't need more successful people.

It needs more leaders who inspire change.

And YOU are meant to be one of them.

Your CEO Journey Starts NOW

No more excuses.
No more waiting.
No more playing small.

The **time to step up** is NOW.

You are the CEO of your life.
You have the power to create your future.
You are capable of leading, impacting, and thriving.

So:

Start leading.
Start taking action.
Start building your legacy.

Because the world is waiting for YOU.

Key Takeaways from the Epilogue

✓ **Your life is your business—take full ownership.**
✓ **Every choice you make determines your future.**
✓ **The greatest investment you will ever make is in yourself.**
✓ **Success is about impact, not just personal gain.**
✓ **Start today—your legacy is built one decision at a time.**

So, let me ask you one last time:

Will you step up and be the CEO of your life?

Because the **journey starts now**.

See you at the top!

CEO LIFE PLAN WORKBOOK

Your Personal Guide to Taking Action

Congratulations on completing this book! But remember, reading alone is not enough—**action** is what leads to transformation.

This **CEO Life Plan Workbook** is designed to help you:

✓ **Clarify your vision for success**
✓ **Identify areas for growth**
✓ **Set actionable goals**
✓ **Create a plan for your future**

Take your time to go through each section thoughtfully. **Be honest with yourself, dream big, and commit to taking action.**

SECTION 1: SELF-ASSESSMENT – WHERE ARE YOU NOW?

Before you **move forward**, you need to **know where you stand**.

This section is about **self-awareness**, **reflection**, and **honest evaluation**.

Why is this important?

Because **growth starts with clarity**. If you don't know where you are, you can't **create a roadmap** to where you want to be.

How to Use This Self-Assessment

✓ **Be honest with yourself** – This is a personal exercise. No one will see your answers.

✓ **Write everything down** – Don't just think about your answers. Write them down in a journal or document.

✓ **Take your time** – Self-awareness is powerful, but it requires reflection.

Let's begin.

1. Personal Growth: Understanding Your Strengths and Weaknesses

Self-improvement starts with **knowing what you're good at** and **what you need to work on**.

Exercise: Identify Your Strengths and Areas for Improvement

Question 1: What are my top 3 strengths?

Think about the **qualities, skills, or abilities** that make you **stand out**.

These could be:

✓ Skills (e.g. public speaking, writing, problem-solving)
✓ Traits (e.g. resilience, determination, empathy)
✓ Habits (e.g. discipline, consistency, learning mindset)

Example:

- **Strength #1:** I am great at **communicating my ideas clearly.**
- **Strength #2:** I am **resilient** and bounce back quickly from setbacks.
- **Strength #3:** I am a **natural leader,** and people trust me to guide them.

Why is this important?

Because knowing your strengths helps you **leverage them** for success.

TIP: Once you identify your strengths, think about how you can **maximize** them in your career, business, or personal life.

Question 2: What are the 3 areas I need to improve?

No one is perfect, and growth happens when we **identify and address our weaknesses**.

These could be:

✓ Skills you lack (e.g. financial literacy, time management)
✓ Habits that hold you back (e.g. procrastination, lack of focus)
✓ Emotional or mindset challenges (e.g. self-doubt, fear of failure)

Example:

- **Improvement Area #1:** I need to improve my **time management** to be more productive.
- **Improvement Area #2:** I struggle with **public speaking** and must practice expressing myself more confidently.
- **Improvement Area #3:** I often second-guess myself and let **fear of failure** stop me from taking action.

Why is this important?

Because identifying your weak areas helps you **create a plan** for improvement.

TIP: Pick one area to focus on first and take **small daily actions** to improve.

2. Breaking Free from Limiting Beliefs

Limiting beliefs are **negative thoughts** or **self-doubts** that **hold you back** from achieving your full potential.

Question 3: What limiting beliefs are holding me back?

These could be:

✓ Fear-based thoughts (e.g., "I'm not good enough.")
✓ Negative self-talk (e.g., "I always fail at new things.")
✓ Beliefs about money, success, or leadership (e.g., "Success is only for lucky people.")

Example of Limiting Beliefs and How to Overcome Them:

✗ **Belief:** "I'm not smart enough to start a business."
✅ **New Mindset:** "I can learn the skills I need to succeed. Every successful entrepreneur started somewhere."
✗ **Belief:** "I'm too old/too young to succeed."
✅ **New Mindset:** "Success has no age limit. If I take action now, I will be ahead in the future."
✗ **Belief:** "I don't have enough time to chase my dreams."
✅ **New Mindset:** "I control my time. If I prioritize, I can make time for what matters."

Why is this important?

Because **your thoughts shape your reality**. If you believe you **can't**, you won't even try.

TIP: Replace every limiting belief with an **empowering statement** that supports your growth.

Final Reflection: Your Personal Growth Blueprint

Now that you've done this self-assessment, what's next?

✅ **Celebrate your strengths** – Use them to your advantage.
✅ **Commit to improving one weakness at a time** – Small progress leads to big results.
✅ **Rewire your mindset** – Turn limiting beliefs into empowering beliefs.

ACTION STEP: Write down **one specific action** you will take this week to improve yourself.

✔ **Example:** "I will dedicate 30 minutes daily to reading books on financial literacy."

Your Success Starts With Self-Awareness

You can't fix what you don't acknowledge.
You can't grow if you don't challenge yourself.
The first step to success is knowing where you are—and where you want to go.
Take this self-assessment seriously and use it as a foundation to make real changes.

Because the best investment you will ever make is in yourself.

2. Career and Financial Goals: Designing a Path to Stability and Growth

Your **career and financial success** don't happen by accident. They are the **results of clear goals, strategic decisions, and disciplined action.**

Why is this important?

Because **financial freedom gives you choices**—the ability to live life on your own terms, pursue your passions, and take control of your future. This self-assessment will help you **evaluate your current situation** and identify the **next steps toward financial growth.**

Am I Happy with My Current Job or Business? Why or Why Not?

The first step to career growth is **honest reflection.**

Ask yourself:

✓ Do I feel **excited** about my work, or do I just do it for the paycheck?
✓ Does my job **align with my long-term goals**?
✓ Do I feel **challenged and valued**, or am I stuck in a routine?

Exercise: Career Satisfaction Check-In

Example Responses:

✓ **I love my job because I get to help people, develop new skills, and grow in my industry.**
✓ **I feel stuck because I'm not learning anything new and don't see opportunities for advancement.**
✓ **I run a business but constantly feel overwhelmed because I don't have the right systems in place.**

Why is this important?

Because **your work takes up a large portion of your life**, you deserve to spend that time doing something meaningful, fulfilling, and financially rewarding.

TIP: If you're unhappy, start exploring ways to pivot—whether through a career change, new skills, or business improvements.

What Is My Biggest Financial Challenge Right Now?

Your financial situation directly affects your quality of life.

Take a moment to identify what's holding you back.

Is it:

✓ **Living paycheck to paycheck** with no savings?
✓ **Lack of financial literacy**—not knowing how to budget, save, or invest?
✓ **Debt** that keeps growing no matter what you do?
✓ **No clear plan** for long-term financial security?

Exercise: Identify Your Financial Roadblocks

Example Responses:

✗ "I struggle with saving money because I have too many expenses."
✗ "I have a lot of debt, and I don't know where to start paying it off."
✗ "I don't have a plan for retirement, and that worries me."

Why is this important?

Because **you can't fix what you don't acknowledge**. You can only start working on a solution when you identify your biggest financial challenge.

TIP: Break your challenge down into **small, actionable steps**.

✓ If you have **debt**, create a **realistic repayment plan**.

✓ If you **struggle with saving**, automate your savings so it happens **before you spend**.

✓ If you **lack financial knowledge**, commit to reading **one finance book per month**.

Do I Have Multiple Income Streams? If Not, What Steps Can I Take to Create Them?

Why is this important?

Because relying on **one source of income** is **risky**.

✓ If you lose your job or business slows down, how will you survive?

✓ How will you build long-term wealth with just a single paycheck?

Exercise: Evaluate Your Income Streams

Question: How many sources of income do I currently have?

Example Responses:

◇ **I have a full-time job and a side hustle selling online.**

◇ **I only have my 9-to-5 job, and if I lost it, I would struggle financially.**

◇ **I have investments, but I don't know if they're generating enough passive income.**

If you ONLY have one income stream, it's time to create a plan for multiple streams.

How to Start Creating Multiple Income Streams:

✓ **Start a side hustle** – Freelancing, consulting, or selling online.

✓ **Invest** – Stocks, real estate, or other assets that appreciate in value.

✓ **Create passive income** – Digital products, rental properties, or affiliate marketing.

✓ **Develop new skills** – Learn high-income skills (e.g. digital marketing, coding, sales).

Your goal should be to make money even when you're not actively working.

Final Reflection: Your Career and Financial Growth Plan

Now that you've done this self-assessment, what's next?

✓ **If you love your job, find ways to grow within your field.**
✓ **If you're unhappy, start planning your exit strategy.**
✓ **If finances stress you out, commit to learning and applying new strategies.**
✓ **If you only have one income source, work on creating multiple streams.**

ACTION STEP: Write down one financial or career goal and one small action step to take this week.

✓ **Example:** "I will set aside £50 from each paycheck to build an emergency fund."

Your Financial Freedom Starts With the Intention

**You don't have to stay in the same financial situation forever.
You can create a career that excites and fulfills you.**

You can build wealth and financial security, but only if you take action.

Take this self-assessment seriously and use it as a foundation to make real changes.

Because your financial future is in your hands.

3. Relationships and Environment: Who Are You Surrounding Yourself With?

Your **relationships** and **environment** play a significant role in shaping your mindset, motivation, and success.

Why is this important?

Because **your surroundings influence your future**.

If you spend time with **negative, unmotivated people**, you'll absorb their energy.

If you surround yourself with **ambitious, growth-driven people**, you'll rise to their level.

This self-assessment will help you **evaluate your social circle and environment**—and identify whether they are helping or hindering your growth.

Who Are the 5 People I Spend the Most Time With? Are They Lifting Me Up or Holding Me Back?

Think about your closest relationships.

✓ Who do you talk to daily or weekly?
✓ Who influences your thoughts, habits, and mindset?
✓ Do they **challenge you to improve** or **keep you stuck in the past**?

Exercise: Evaluate Your Inner Circle

Write down the 5 people you spend the most time with.

Example:

John – My best friend; always encourages me to push forward and take risks.

Lisa – My coworker; complains a lot about work and discourages ambition.

Mike – A mentor; gives valuable advice on business and personal growth.

Sarah – A family member; supportive but often stuck in negative thinking.

David – My business partner is driven, focused, and challenges me to improve.

Now ask yourself:

✓ Who is **lifting me up** and pushing me toward success?
✓ Who is **holding me back** with negativity, fear, or complacency?

TIP: If someone in your circle constantly drains **your energy**, consider **limiting your time with them.**

You don't have to **cut people off completely**, but you **can** choose to **prioritize relationships that inspire and elevate you.**

Am I Surrounding Myself with People Who Encourage Growth?

Growth is contagious.

When you **surround yourself with people who are constantly learning, improving, and striving for success**, it **motivates you to do the same.**

Ask yourself:

✓ Do my friends and colleagues discuss **goals, success, and possibilities**—or do they focus on gossip, drama, and negativity?

✓ Are the people around me **goal-oriented and driven**, or do they **settle for mediocrity?**

✓ Do I feel **motivated and inspired** after spending time with them, or do I feel **drained and discouraged**?

Exercise: Audit Your Social Environment

Example Responses:

✓ **I am part of a mastermind group where we push each other to achieve our goals.**

✓ **I attend networking events to meet successful and inspiring individuals.**

✓ **Most of my friends just complain about life but don't take action to change it.**

Why is this important?

Because **your success is often determined by the standards of your environment.**

TIP: If your circle isn't encouraging growth, start looking for new connections:

✓ **Join networking groups** in your industry.
✓ **Attend personal development workshops** and conferences.
✓ **Engage with people who have already achieved what you aspire to.**

If you want to **grow**, you need to **be in a space where growth is the norm.**

Who Are My Mentors, and How Often Do I Seek Their Guidance?

Everyone needs a mentor.

No matter how smart, talented, or ambitious you are, there will always be **someone ahead of you** who has **already walked your path.**

Ask yourself:

✓ Who are the **mentors, coaches, or role models** I learn from?
✓ How often do I **seek their advice or guidance**?
✓ Am I **taking action on what I learn**, or just absorbing information without implementation?

Exercise: Identify Your Mentors and Learning Sources

Example Responses:

✅ **My mentor is a successful entrepreneur, and I meet with him once a month for advice.**
✅ **I follow industry leaders through books, podcasts, and online courses.**
✅ **I don't have a direct mentor yet, but I am actively seeking one.**

Why is this important?

Because **mentorship accelerates success.**

✓ A good mentor **saves you years of trial and error.**
✓ They help you **avoid costly mistakes.**
✓ They give you **insights and strategies** that took them years to learn.

TIP: If you don't have a mentor yet, start looking for one:

✓ Join **mentorship programs** in your industry.
✓ Attend **networking events** and seek connections with experienced professionals.
✓ Find **virtual mentors** through books, podcasts, and online courses.

Final Reflection: Your Relationship and Environment Blueprint

Now that you've done this self-assessment, what's next?

✅ **If your circle isn't pushing you forward, surround yourself with high-achievers.**

✅ **If you don't have a mentor, start seeking one today.**

✅ **If your environment isn't encouraging growth, change it.**

ACTION STEP: Write down **one specific action** you will take this week to improve your social circle.

✓ **Example:** "I will reach out to a potential mentor and schedule a call."

Your Environment Shapes Your Future

You can't grow in a toxic environment.
You can't succeed if your circle discourages ambition.

The right people will push you further than you could ever go alone.

Take this self-assessment seriously and start building relationships that fuel your growth.

Because success is a team effort.

4. Faith and Purpose: Strengthening Your Spiritual Foundation

Your **faith and purpose** are the foundation for everything you do in life.

Why is this important?

Because when you have **clarity in your values and purpose**, you:

✓ **Make better decisions**
✓ **Handle challenges with resilience**
✓ **Find fulfillment beyond just financial success**

This self-assessment will help you **reflect on your spiritual life, personal values, and alignment with your true purpose.**

How Strong Is My Spiritual Foundation?

Your spiritual foundation is the core of your inner strength.

Regardless of religious beliefs, **faith** is about:

✓ Finding **peace** in difficult times
✓ Having **hope** for the future
✓ Trusting that your life has **meaning and direction**

Exercise: Evaluate Your Spiritual Connection

Ask yourself:

✓ Do I take time to **reflect, pray, or meditate** daily?
✓ When challenges arise, do I **lean on faith or rely only on logic**?
✓ Do I feel **connected to a greater purpose**, or do I often feel lost?

Example Responses:

✓ **I have a strong faith, which helps me stay calm and focused in difficult times.**
✓ **I struggle with spirituality because I've been hurt in the past, but I want to rebuild my faith.**
✓ **I feel disconnected but want to start practicing gratitude and prayer again.**

Why is this important?

Because **without faith, challenges feel overwhelming.**

TIP: If you want to **strengthen your spiritual foundation**, try:

✓ Reading **books or scriptures** that align with your faith
✓ Practicing **daily gratitude** for small and big blessings

✓ Joining a **faith-based community** for support

What Values Do I Want to Live By?

Your values guide your decisions and actions.

Ask yourself:

✓ What **principles and morals** are most important to me?
✓ Am I **living according to my values**, or am I compromising them?
✓ How do I want to be **remembered** by my family, friends, and community?

Exercise: Identify Your Core Values

Example Responses:

✅ **Integrity** – I want to be honest and do the right thing, even when no one is watching.
✅ **Growth** – I want to keep learning and improving every day.
✅ **Generosity** – I want to share my blessings with others and give back.

Why is this important?

Because **when you live by your values, you experience inner peace and fulfillment.**

TIP: Write down your values and review them regularly to ensure that your decisions align with them.

Am I Aligned with My Purpose in Life?

Your purpose is your "why"—the reason you wake up every day with motivation.

Ask yourself:

✓ Do I feel like my daily work and actions contribute to a **greater purpose?**

✓ When I imagine my future, do I feel **excited or empty?**

✓ Am I using my skills and talents to **serve others and create impact?**

Exercise: Find Your Purpose

Example Responses:

✓ **I love what I do and know I'm making a difference.**

✓ **I feel like I'm just existing but want to find something meaningful.**

✓ **I know my purpose, but I've been too afraid to pursue it fully.**

Why is this important?

Because **without purpose, success feels meaningless.**

TIP: If you feel **disconnected from your purpose,** start by:

✓ Exploring **what you're naturally good at**

✓ Asking **how you can serve others with your talents**

✓ Taking small steps toward a **passion-driven life**

Final Reflection: Your Faith and Purpose Blueprint

Now that you've done this self-assessment, what's next?

✓ If you feel disconnected from your faith, take small steps to reconnect.

✓ **If you aren't living by your values, make daily choices that reflect them.**

✓ **If you feel lost in your purpose, explore what excites and fulfills you.**

ACTION STEP: Write down one specific action you will take this week to strengthen your faith and purpose.

✓ **Example:** "I will start my mornings with 5 minutes of gratitude and prayer."

Your Faith and Purpose Shape Everything Else

A strong spiritual foundation keeps you grounded in hard times.
Living by your values builds self-respect and inner peace.
Discovering your purpose gives your life true meaning.
Take this self-assessment seriously and use it as a guide to realigning your life.

Because true success is not just about wealth but about fulfillment, impact, and purpose.

SECTION 2: CLARIFY YOUR VISION – WHERE DO YOU WANT TO BE?

Why is this important?

Because **you can't hit a target you can't see.**

If you don't have a clear vision of where you want to be in 5 years, **you'll drift through life without direction. This exercise will help you design your ideal future—one that excites and fulfills you.**

Take your time, dream big, and write **everything down.**

1. Personal and Spiritual Growth: Who Are You Becoming?

Your **growth** determines your **success.**

In 5 years, do you want to be:

✓ More confident?
✓ More disciplined?

✓ More spiritually connected?

Ask yourself:

✓ **What kind of person do I want to become?**
✓ **What skills do I want to master?**
✓ **How do I want to think, act, and feel daily?**

How Do I See Myself in 5 Years?

Close your eyes and imagine your ideal self.

Example Response:

✓ **In 5 years, I see myself as a confident, self-disciplined, and spiritually strong person. I am living a life of purpose, helping others grow while continuously improving myself. I wake up feeling energized and excited about my day.**

Why is this important?

Because **your vision shapes your reality**. If you don't define who you want to become, you'll end up wherever life takes you.

TIP: Write a **detailed description** of your future self. **Visualize it as if it's already happening.**

What Kind of Mindset Do I Want to Develop?

Your mindset controls your success.

If you want to succeed, you need to:

✓ **Let go of limiting beliefs**
✓ **Adopt a success-oriented mindset**
✓ **Stay resilient in the face of challenges**

Ask yourself:

✓ **Do I want a mindset of abundance or scarcity?**
✓ **Do I want to be driven by fear or by faith?**
✓ **Do I want to embrace challenges or avoid them?**

Example Response:

◇ **In 5 years, I will have a mindset of abundance and gratitude. I will embrace challenges as opportunities to grow and will no longer let fear hold me back. I will think big, take bold actions, and trust in my abilities.**

Why is this important?

Because **your thoughts shape your actions, and your actions shape your results**.

TIP: Write down **one belief** you must change today to develop your desired mindset.

✓ **Example:** "I will stop thinking that success is for 'other people' and start believing that I am just as capable as anyone else."

What Habits Do I Need to Build or Break?

Your habits determine your future.

Ask yourself:

✓ What **positive habits** do I need to build to reach my goals?
✓ What **negative habits** are holding me back?
✓ How will I stay **consistent** in improving my habits?

Exercise: Identify Key Habits

Example Response:

✔ **Habits to Build:**

✔ Wake up early and start my day with prayer/meditation

✔ Read personal development books for 30 minutes daily

✔ Exercise at least 4 times a week

✔ Manage my time effectively and eliminate distractions

✔ **Habits to Break:**

✖ Procrastinating and overthinking

✖ Wasting hours on social media

✖ Complaining instead of taking action

✖ Doubting my own abilities

Why is this important?

Because **your habits create your reality**. Small daily actions determine whether you will **succeed or stay stuck**.

TIP: Pick **one habit to improve** this week and commit to it daily.

✔ **Example:** "I will replace 30 minutes of social media scrolling with reading a personal growth book."

Final Reflection: Your Personal and Spiritual Growth Plan

Now that you've clarified your vision, what's next?

✔ **If you want to be confident, start practicing confidence daily.**
✔ **If you want to be disciplined, create routines that build self-discipline.**
✔ **If you want to be spiritually strong, dedicate time to faith and reflection.**

ACTION STEP: Write down **one specific action** you will take this week to move closer to your five-year vision.

✓ **Example:** "I will wake up 30 minutes earlier every day to pray, journal, and plan my day."

Your Growth is in Your Hands

The next 5 years will pass whether you take action or not.
The question is—will you be the same person you are today, or will you have grown into your best self?
Take this exercise seriously and start building the future you desire.

Because the best version of you is waiting—you just have to start today.

2. Career & Business Goals: Designing Your Future Success

Why is this important?

Because **if you don't have a vision for your career or business, you will settle for less than you deserve.**

This self-assessment will help you **clarify where you want to be, how much you want to earn, and what skills you need to develop to get there.**

Take your time, think big, and write **everything down**.

What Position or Business Do I Want to Be In?

Ask yourself:

✓ **Am I happy in my current job or business?**
✓ **Do I see myself growing in my current field, or do I want to transition into something new?**
✓ **What position, title, or business goal excites me the most?**

Exercise: Visualize Your Future Career or Business

Example Responses:

✓ **Career Path:** "In 5 years, I want to be a Senior Manager in my company, leading a team and making high-level business decisions."

✓ **Entrepreneurial Path:** "I want to own a successful online business that generates passive income, so I have the freedom to travel and work from anywhere."

✓ **Freelancer Path:** "I want to be a highly paid consultant in my industry, offering expert services on my own terms."

Why is this important?

Because **when you define where you want to go, you create a clear path to get there.**

TIP: Write down your **ideal position or business idea in detail—** what you do daily, how you feel, and what success looks like for you.

How Much Income Do I Want to Earn?

Money gives you choices and freedom.

Your income goals should match the **lifestyle and impact you want to create.**

Ask yourself:

✓ How much do I want to earn per month or year?
✓ What income level would give me financial security and freedom?
✓ How can I increase my earning potential through career growth, business, or investments?

Exercise: Set Your Income Goals

Example Responses:

✅ **Career Path:** "In 5 years, I want to earn £150,000 annually as a corporate executive."

✅ **Entrepreneurial Path:** "I want my business to generate £500,000 per year in revenue, with at least 50% in profit."

✅ **Side Hustle Path:** "I want to create multiple streams of income that generate an extra £5,000 per month outside of my main job."

Why is this important?

Because **if you don't set financial goals, you will accept whatever income comes your way.**

TIP: Set **specific** and **realistic** income goals that challenge you to grow while keeping them achievable with the right plan.

What Skills or Knowledge Do I Need to Get There?

Your skills determine your earning potential.

If you want to **increase your income**, you need to **increase your value**.

Ask yourself:

✓ **What skills do I need to succeed in my ideal career or business?**
✓ **What do top professionals in my field know that I don't?**
✓ **What courses, training, or mentorship can help me level up?**

Exercise: Identify Your Growth Areas

Example Responses:

✅ **Career Path:** "I need to improve my leadership skills, learn strategic planning, and obtain a professional certification."

✔ **Entrepreneurial Path:** "I must master digital marketing, financial management, and customer acquisition strategies."

✔ **Freelancer Path:** "I need to develop expertise in personal branding, sales, and networking to attract high-paying clients."

Why is this important?

Because **you don't get paid for time, you get paid for the value you bring to the marketplace.**

TIP: Make a list of **books, courses, and mentors** to help you gain the skills you need to reach your career or business goals.

Final Reflection: Your Career and Business Blueprint

Now that you've clarified your vision, what's next?

✔ **If you want a higher position, develop leadership and business skills.**

✔ **If you want to increase your income, start learning how to create multiple revenue streams.**

✔ **If you want to switch careers, start building the skills and network for your new industry.**

ACTION STEP: Write down **one specific action** you will take this week to move closer to your five-year career and financial goal.

✔ **Example:** "I will enroll in an online course on business strategy to develop my leadership skills."

Your Future Success Starts With Clarity & Action

If you don't define your goals, someone else will define them for you.
The best way to predict your future is to create it.

Take this self-assessment seriously and start taking steps today to build your desired career and income.

Because taking the first step is essential to making your dream career or business a reality.

3. Relationships and Support System: Building a Strong Network for Growth

Why is this important?

Because **your success is not just about what you do but also about who you surround yourself with.**

Your **relationships, friendships, mentors, and community** play a **huge role** in your growth, happiness, and overall success.

This self-assessment will help you **clarify who you need in your life, how to nurture important relationships, and how to contribute to your community and faith.**

Who Do I Want to Surround Myself With?

Your circle determines your level of success.

Ask yourself:

✓ Who inspires me to **grow, push past my limits, and become a better person?**
✓ Do my current relationships **lift me up or hold me back?**
✓ Who do I need to **spend more time with, and who do I need to distance myself from?**

Exercise: Identify Your Ideal Inner Circle

Example Responses:

✓ **Mentors:** "I want to be surrounded by people who are ahead of me in life and business, so I can learn from their experiences."

✓ **Friends:** "I want to build strong friendships with people who support my goals and push me to grow."

✓ **Peers:** "I want to connect with like-minded individuals who share my ambition and values."

Why is this important?

Because **your environment shapes your mindset**. If you spend time with people who **think big, work hard, and support each other**, you will do the same.

TIP: Identify 3 people you want to **build stronger connections with** and reach out to them this week.

How Will I Invest in My Marriage, Friendships, and Mentors?

Great relationships don't happen by accident; they require effort and intentionality.

Ask yourself:

✓ How can I **be more present** and show appreciation in my relationships?

✓ What habits can I build to **strengthen my marriage or close friendships?**

✓ How can I **stay connected and learn from my mentors consistently?**

Exercise: Relationship Investment Plan

Example Responses:

✅ **Marriage/Partner:** "I will schedule regular date nights and communicate more openly with my spouse."

✅ **Friendships:** "I will reach out to close friends weekly and make time for meaningful conversations."

✅ **Mentors:** "I will ask my mentor for monthly check-ins and apply their advice consistently."

Why is this important?

Because **strong relationships create a strong foundation for success.**

TIP: Make a habit of **expressing gratitude** to the important people in your life—small acts of kindness go a long way.

How Will I Contribute to My Community and Faith Group?

True success isn't just about what you achieve—it's about the impact you make.

Ask yourself:

✔ How can I **use my skills and resources** to help others?
✔ How can I **give back** to my faith group, local community, or cause I believe in?

✔ What small, consistent actions can I take to **make a difference?**

Exercise: Contribution and Impact Plan

Example Responses:

✅ **Faith Group:** "I will volunteer once a month at my church and participate in group discussions to grow spiritually."

✔ **Community Involvement:** "I will mentor young professionals and guide them in their career journeys."

✔ **Giving Back:** "I will donate a percentage of my income to a cause that matters to me."

Why is this important?

Because **life is more meaningful when we give back**. Helping others **strengthens your own sense of purpose and fulfillment.**

TIP: Start small—**a simple act of kindness, a donation, or volunteering an hour can have a big impact.**

Final Reflection: Your Relationship and Support System Plan

Now that you've clarified your vision, what's next?

✔ **If you need better influences, seek high-level mentors and friends.**
✔ **If you want stronger relationships, be more intentional about investing in them.**
✔ **If you want to make an impact, take one small step this week toward serving your community.**

ACTION STEP: Write down **one specific action** you will take this week to improve your relationships and support system.

✔ **Example:** "I will schedule a mentorship call with a successful entrepreneur I admire."

Your Success Is a Team Effort

You are the average of the 5 people you spend the most time with. Your relationships determine your happiness, mindset, and success. Your legacy is built through the impact you make in your community.

Take this self-assessment seriously and start surrounding yourself with the right people, investing in relationships, and giving back.

Because success is not just about personal achievement—it's about lifting others up with you.

4. Legacy and Impact: Creating a Meaningful Life That Lasts

Why is this important?

Because at the end of your life, **what will truly matter?**

✓ The **money you made?**
✓ The **titles you held?**
✓ The **things you owned?**
✗ **No.**

What truly matters is:

✓ The **lives you touched.**
✓ The **impact you made.**
✓ The **legacy you left behind.**

This self-assessment will help you **define what kind of legacy you want to build and how you can start making a lasting impact today.**

What Do I Want to Be Remembered For?

Ask yourself:

✓ When people talk about me after I'm gone, what do I want them to say?
✓ How do I want my family, friends, and community to remember me?
✓ What kind of influence do I want to leave behind?

Exercise: Write Your Legacy Statement

Example Responses:

☑ I want to be remembered as a leader who inspired and empowered others to believe in themselves and take action.

☑ I want to be known as someone who was kind, generous, and always willing to help those in need.

☑ I want to leave a legacy of wisdom, leadership, and service, helping people overcome financial struggles and build a life they love.

Why is this important?

Because **your actions today shape how people will remember you tomorrow.**

TIP: Write down a **one-sentence legacy statement** that defines how you want to be remembered. Then, start living according to it **now.**

How Will I Give Back to Others?

Success is not just about personal gain; it's about how many lives you uplift.

Ask yourself:

✓ How can I use my **skills, time, or resources** to serve others?
✓ Can I **mentor, teach, or inspire** someone who is on the journey I once traveled?
✓ How can I use my career or business to **make a positive difference in the world?**

Exercise: Create a Contribution Plan

Example Responses:

✓ I will mentor young professionals and guide them in their career journeys.

✓ I will create a foundation to support education for underprivileged students.

✓ I will dedicate one day a month to volunteer work in my community.

Why is this important?

Because **true fulfillment comes from serving others.**

TIP: Start small—**help one person, volunteer a few hours, or donate to a cause that matters to you.**

What Steps Can I Take Now to Build My Legacy?

Your legacy is built one decision at a time.

Ask yourself:

✓ What actions can I take **today** to start building my legacy?
✓ What habits do I need to form to live by my values?
✓ What kind of work or projects can I start that will have a lasting impact?

Exercise: Identify Legacy-Building Actions

Example Responses:

✓ I will start writing a book that shares my life lessons and wisdom with others.

✓ I will begin recording videos and podcasts to inspire people through my experiences.

☑ I will create a scholarship program to help students from disadvantaged backgrounds.

Why is this important?

Because **if you don't start now, your legacy will only exist as an idea—not a reality.**

TIP: Identify **one step** you can take this week toward building your legacy and take action immediately.

Final Reflection: Your Legacy and Impact Blueprint

Now that you've clarified your vision, what's next?

☑ **If you want to be remembered as a leader, start leading today.**
☑ **If you want to give back, start small—help one person.**
☑ **If you want to leave a lasting impact, start creating something bigger than yourself.**

ACTION STEP: Write down **one specific action** you will take this week to start building your legacy.

✓ **Example:** "I will mentor one person this month and guide them in their career."

Your Legacy Begins Today

Legacy isn't something you leave behind when you die; it's something you build while you live. Every action, every decision, every impact you make today contributes to how you will be remembered.

The question is: Are you living in a way that reflects the legacy you want to leave?

Take this self-assessment seriously and start shaping your legacy now.

Because success is temporary, but the impact you make on others will last forever.

SECTION 3: THE CEO ACTION PLAN – TAKING CHARGE OF YOUR LIFE

Now that you've **assessed where you are** and **clarified your vision**, it's time to **create an action plan** to turn your dreams into reality.

Why is this important?

Because **without action, even the best plans are just ideas**.

The **CEO of a company** doesn't just dream—they **set clear goals and execute a plan to achieve them**.

Now, it's time for you to do the same.

Step 1: Set Your Top 3 Goals for the Next 12 Months

Define your most important goals for the year.

Ask yourself:

✓ **What are the 3 most important achievements I want to accomplish?**
✓ **Which areas of my life need the most improvement?**
✓ **What goals will create the biggest impact on my career, finances, and personal growth?**

✅ **Career/Business Goal:** ________________

Example Goals:

✅ "Get promoted to a leadership role within my company."
✅ "Launch my online business and generate £5,000/month in revenue."
✅ "Expand my business and hire my first employee."

✅ "Build a personal brand and grow my LinkedIn network to 10,000 followers."

Why is this important?

Because **if you don't set career or business goals, you'll stay in the same place year after year**.

TIP: Make your goal **specific, measurable, and time-bound** (SMART).

✓ **Example:** Instead of saying, *"Grow my business,"* say:

Increase business revenue to £100,000 by the end of the year by expanding services and implementing digital marketing.

✅ **Financial Goal:** ______________

Example Goals:

✅ "Save £10,000 for an emergency fund."
✅ "Pay off £5,000 in debt by the end of the year."
✅ "Increase my income by 30% through a new side hustle."
✅ "Invest in stocks or real estate to create passive income."

Why is this important?

Because **financial stability gives you freedom, security, and the ability to create opportunities.**

TIP: Break your financial goal down into smaller, **actionable steps**.

✓ **Example:** Instead of saying, *"Save money,"* say:

Save £500 per month by reducing unnecessary expenses and increasing my side income.

✅ **Personal/Spiritual Goal:** ______________

Example Goals:

✓ Wake up at 5 AM daily to pray, journal, and plan my day.

✓ Read 12 books on personal growth, leadership, and spirituality.

✓ Join a faith-based group and actively participate in community service.

✓ Improve my health by exercising 4 times weekly and eating healthier meals.

Why is this important?

Because **personal and spiritual growth leads to a more fulfilling, balanced, and purpose-driven life.**

TIP: Identify daily or weekly habits to help you achieve your goal.

✓ **Example:** Instead of saying, *"Improve my spiritual life,"* say:

I will spend 15 minutes praying or meditating every morning before starting my day.

Final Reflection: Your CEO Roadmap for the Next 12 Months

Now that you've set your top 3 goals, what's next?

✓ **Write them down and review them daily.**
✓ **Break them into smaller action steps.**
✓ **Track your progress and adjust when needed.**

ACTION STEP: Write down one small action you will take **this week** to move closer to your top 3 goals.

✓ **Example:**

Career Goal: "Schedule a meeting with my boss to discuss my growth plan."

Financial Goal Set up an automatic savings transfer of $100 per month."

Personal Goal: "Wake up 30 minutes earlier to start a morning routine."

Your Success Depends on the Actions You Take Today

A goal without a plan is just a wish.

A dream without action remains a fantasy.

If you want to transform your life, take charge like a CEO.

Take this exercise seriously, commit to your goals, and execute your action plan daily.

Because the next 12 months will either be the same as the last or they will be your breakthrough year. The choice is yours.

Step 2: Break It Down into Small Steps

Why is this important?

Because **big goals can feel overwhelming**—but when you break them down into **small, achievable steps**, they become manageable.

Think of your **goal** as a **mountain** and each **action step** as a **step on the path to the top.**

How to Do This:

✓ For each of your **top 3 goals**, write **3 specific actions** you will take in the next 30 days.

✓ These actions should be **clear, simple, and achievable** within the given time frame.

✓ They should **move you closer** to achieving the overall goal.

✅ **Goal 1 Action Steps: (Career/Business Goal)**

Example Goal: "Get promoted to a leadership role within my company."

✅ **Action Step 1:** Schedule a meeting with your manager to discuss your career growth plan.

✅ **Action Step 2:** Take an online leadership course to improve your management skills.

✅ **Action Step 3:** Offer to lead a small project at work to showcase your leadership abilities.

Why is this important?

Because **small, intentional actions add up to big results over time.**

TIP: Focus on **consistent progress**, not perfection.

✅ **Goal 2 Action Steps: (Financial Goal)**

Example Goal: "Save £10,000 for an emergency fund."

✅ **Action Step 1:** Set up an automatic transfer of £500 per month into a savings account.

✅ **Action Step 2:** Reduce unnecessary expenses (e.g., eating out, subscriptions) and track spending.

✅ **Action Step 3:** Start a small side hustle to increase my income.

Why is this important?

Because **financial freedom starts with small daily money habits.**

TIP: If saving feels difficult, start small—**even saving £10 a day adds up over time.**

✅ **Goal 3 Action Steps: (Personal/Spiritual Goal)**

Example Goal: "Wake up at 5 am daily to pray, journal, and plan my day."

✅ **Action Step 1:** Set an alarm 30 minutes earlier than usual and gradually adjust my sleep schedule.

✅ **Action Step 2:** Create a morning routine checklist (prayer, journaling, exercise, goal setting).

✅ **Action Step 3:** Find an accountability partner to check in with daily progress.

Why is this important?

Because **daily habits determine long-term success in personal and spiritual growth.**

TIP: Track your morning routine in a journal or app to stay consistent.

Final Reflection: Your 30-Day Action Plan

Now that you've broken your goals into small steps, what's next?

✅ **Write these action steps somewhere visible**—your planner, phone, or journal.

✅ **Schedule them in your calendar to stay committed.**

✅ **Track your progress weekly and adjust when needed.**

ACTION STEP: Choose **one action from each goal** and do it **within the next 3 days.**

✓ **Example:**

Career Goal: "Enroll in a leadership course today."

Financial Goal: "Set up an automatic savings transfer today."

Personal Goal: "Wake up 30 minutes earlier starting tomorrow."

Success is the Result of Consistent Action

Will you be closer to your dream life a year from now or still stuck in the same place?

The difference is what you do TODAY.

Take this step seriously—because the next 30 days could be the beginning of your breakthrough.

Because the only way to make progress is to start.

Step 3: Identify Potential Challenges & Solutions

Why is this important?

Because **every goal comes with obstacles**—but the people who succeed are the ones who **prepare for challenges in advance.** When you **anticipate roadblocks**, you can **create solutions before they happen,** making it easier to stay on track.

How to Do This:

✓ **Identify 2 main obstacles** that could prevent you from achieving your goals.

✓ **Write down a practical solution** for each obstacle so you can overcome it when it arises.

✓ **Be proactive**—this will help you stay committed when challenges arise.

✅ **Obstacle 1: Lack of Time**

Why this is a challenge:

✓ You might feel **too busy** to work on your goals due to work, family, or other responsibilities.

✓ Time management can be difficult, leading to procrastination.

✅ **Solution:**

✓ **Prioritize tasks** by scheduling time blocks in your calendar.
✓ **Wake up earlier or set specific hours** for focused work on your goals.
✓ **Eliminate distractions** like social media, TV, or unnecessary activities.
✓ **Use productivity tools** like time-blocking apps or planners.

Example:

Goal: "Take an online leadership course."

Solution: "Dedicate 30 minutes every evening before bed to study."

✅ **Obstacle 2: Lack of Motivation & Self-Discipline**

Why this is a challenge:

✓ Some days, you may feel **lazy, discouraged, or unmotivated** to take action.
✓ You might struggle with **consistency** or give up after a few weeks.

✅ **Solution:**

✓ **Find an accountability partner**—someone who will check in on your progress.
✓ **Break goals into smaller steps** to make them feel less overwhelming.
✓ **Celebrate small wins** to stay motivated.
✓ **Remind yourself why you started** by reviewing your vision daily.

Example:

Goal: "Save £10,000 for an emergency fund."

Solution: "Set up an automatic savings transfer so I don't rely on willpower."

Final Reflection: Preparing for Success

Now that you've identified challenges, what's next?

✓ Keep these solutions in mind when obstacles arise.
✓ Plan ahead so setbacks don't stop you.
✓ Stay focused on your long-term vision and keep moving forward.

ACTION STEP: Choose **one solution** and apply it **this week** to stay ahead of potential challenges.

✓ **Example:**

"I will schedule a specific time in my calendar for my goal-related tasks to avoid excuses."

Success Is About Problem-Solving

Challenges will come, but they won't stop you if you plan for them. Winners don't quit when things get hard—they adjust and keep going.
Take this step seriously because preparation is the key to long-term success.
Because when you have a plan for obstacles, nothing can hold you back.

SECTION 4: ACCOUNTABILITY – WHO WILL SUPPORT YOU?

Why is this important?

Because **success is not a solo journey.**

✓ The most successful people have **mentors, accountability partners, and support systems** that keep them focused and motivated.

✓ When you share your goals with **the right people**, they help **push you forward, encourage you, and hold you accountable.**

It's time to identify who will support you on your journey.

✅ **My Mentor:** ________________

Why do you need a mentor?

✓ A mentor is someone **who has already achieved what you want to achieve.**
✓ They **guide, challenge, and help you avoid costly mistakes.**
✓ They provide **valuable feedback and encouragement** when you face challenges.

Ask yourself:

✓ Who do I admire and respect in my industry or field?
✓ Who has experience and wisdom that I can learn from?
✓ Who is willing to mentor me and provide guidance when needed?

Example Responses:

✅ **"My mentor is a senior executive in my company who has been guiding me in leadership development."**
✅ **"I have a business coach who helps me stay accountable for my revenue goals."**
✅ **"I follow an online mentor (through books, podcasts, and courses) and apply their teachings."**

Next Step: If you don't have a mentor yet, **identify someone and reach out to them** this week.

✓ **Example:** "I will send a message to the mentor I admire and ask for a 15-minute conversation."

✅ **Check-in Frequency:** ________________

Why is this important?

✓ Regular **check-ins** keep you **focused and accountable.**

✓ They ensure you **stay on track** with your goals.

✓ They provide **a chance to reflect, adjust, and stay motivated.**

Choose how often you will check in with your mentor:

Example Responses:

✓ **I will check in with my mentor once a month for career/business progress.**

✓ **I will schedule a weekly call with my accountability partner to review my goals.**

✓ **I will track my progress daily and discuss major milestones quarterly.**

Next Step: Schedule **your first check-in today**—put it on your calendar.

✓ **Example:** "I will set up a monthly meeting with my mentor to track my progress."

✓ **My Support System (Spouse, Friends, or Business Partners):**

____

Why is this important?

✓ Your support system keeps **you motivated and encouraged.**

✓ They **remind you of your WHY** when you feel like giving up.

✓ They provide **emotional and mental support** throughout your journey.

Ask yourself:

✓ Who in my life **genuinely supports and believes in me?**

✓ Who will **hold me accountable** when I feel like making excuses?

✓ Who can I rely on for **motivation, advice, and encouragement?**

Example Responses:

✓ **My spouse is my biggest supporter, and we will discuss my goals weekly.**

✓ **I have a group of business partners who keep each other accountable every month.**

✓ **I have a mastermind group that meets every 2 weeks to review our progress.**

Next Step: Tell your support system about your goals and ask for their **encouragement and accountability.**

✓ **Example:** "I will share my goals with my spouse and ask him or her to check in on my progress every Sunday."

Final Reflection: Your Accountability Plan

Now that you've identified your accountability system, what's next?

✓ **If you don't have a mentor, find one this week.**

✓ **If you haven't set a check-in schedule, put it on your calendar now.**

✓ **If you need more support, surround yourself with people who push you to grow.**

ACTION STEP: Choose **one action** to strengthen your accountability system this week.

✓ **Example:** "I will schedule my first accountability check-in with my mentor for next Monday."

Your Support System Will Help You Succeed

You don't have to do this alone—great leaders and achievers always have accountability partners. The right people will challenge,

encourage, and help you stay committed. Your success is more likely when you have a mentor and a strong support system backing you.

Take this step seriously—because having the right support can make all the difference.

Because when you surround yourself with winners, success becomes inevitable.

SECTION 5: COMMITMENT – SIGN YOUR CEO AGREEMENT

Why is this important?

Because **commitment is the bridge between goals and success.**

✓ You can set goals.
✓ You can make action plans.
✓ You can visualize your future.

But **none of it matters unless you fully commit** to doing what it takes to achieve your dreams.

This is your **CEO Agreement**—a **personal contract** with yourself to take ownership of your success, lead your life with intention, and stay disciplined in pursuing your goals.

CEO AGREEMENT

I, (Your Name), commit to taking full ownership of my success.

✓ **I will take action every day to move closer to my goals.**
✓ **I will overcome obstacles with resilience and adaptability.**
✓ **I will create a life of impact, purpose, and financial freedom.**
✓ **I will think, act, and lead like a CEO—because my life is my business.**

Date: _______________

Signature: _______________

FINAL WORDS: YOUR NEXT STEPS

This is not the end of your journey but the beginning of your transformation.

The question is: Will you take action or let another year pass without real change?

✓ Success doesn't happen overnight, but it does happen when you take small, consistent steps every day.
✓ Your future is in your hands.

✓ Your Action Plan from Today

✓ Revisit your goals every morning to stay focused.
✓ Take action—start with ONE small step TODAY.
✓ Track your progress and adjust as needed.
✓ Surround yourself with people who push you to grow.
✓ Stay disciplined—because consistency creates results.

See You at the Top!

You are now officially the CEO of your life.
Go make your vision a reality.
Because the only limits you have are the ones you refuse to break.

References & Citations

Churchill, Winston. (n.d.). Success is not final; failure is not fatal; it is the courage to continue that counts. Retrieved from multiple historical quote sources.

Jobs, Steve. (2005). Commencement Speech at Stanford University.

Maxwell, John C. (n.d.). Dreams don't work unless you do.

Emerson, Ralph Waldo (1841) Essays: First Series.

King, Martin Luther Jr. (n.d.). "If you can't fly, then run; if you can't run, then walk; if you can't walk, then crawl; but whatever you do, you have to keep moving forward."

Fishel, Elizabeth. (n.d.). Sisters: The True Meaning of Family.

Branson, Richard. (n.d.). "Do not be embarrassed by your failures; learn from them and start again."

Disney, Walt. (n.d.). The way to get started is to quit talking and begin doing.

Keller, Helen. (1903). The Story of My Life.

Einstein, Albert. (n.d.). Try not to become a man of success, but rather try to become a man of value.

Sinek, Simon. (2014). Leaders Eat Last: Why Some Teams Pull Together and Others Don't.

Ford, Henry. (n.d.). Whether you think you can or you think you can't – you're right.

Jobs, Steve. (2005). Your time is limited, so don't waste it living someone else's life.

Jefferson, Thomas. (n.d.). "If you want something you've never had, you must be willing to do something you've never done." Retrieved from multiple historical quote sources.

www.ingramcontent.com/pod-product-compliance
Lightning Source LLC
Chambersburg PA
CBHW021223130726
47988CB00002B/800